# Glenn Alterman

**ALLWORTH PRESS**
NEW YORK

*This book is dedicated to*
*my former acting teachers:*

Wynn Handman
Michael Howard
Terry Schreiber
Harold Guskin
Larry Moss

© 1998 Glenn Alterman

Published by Allworth Press
An imprint of Allworth Communications
10 East 23rd Street, New York, NY 10010

Cover design by Douglas Designs, New York, NY

Book design by Sharp Des!gns, Inc., Lansing, MI

ISBN: 1-880559-97-8

Library of Congress Catalog Card Number: 98-70412

Printed in Canada

# Contents

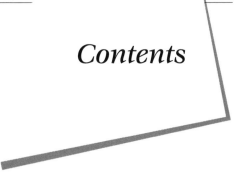

# Acknowledgments

I wish to thank the following people for their help with this book: Bunny Levine, David Zema, Eva Charney, Carlotta Bogavianos, Linda Chapman (New York Theater Workshop), Merle Frimark, Doug Barron, Herbert Rubens, Spider Duncan Christopher, Michael Warren Powell, Lee K. Bohlen, Karen Kayser, Alan Nusbaum, Joe Stern (the Mattrix Theater), Richard Bauman, Martin Gage, John Wasser, Shirley Rich—and all of the photographers, casting directors, artistic directors of theater companies, publicists, reproduction studio owners, videographers, actors, and the many others who granted interviews, took my phone calls, and provided the invaluable information that aided in the writing of this book.

Thank you all very much.

# Preface

**Promote** 1. to advance in station, rank, or honor. 2. to contribute to the growth or prosperity of: further. 3. To help bring into being: launch

I decided to write this book after noticing that many of my actor friends, although very talented, were constantly unemployed. I knew for a fact that they were out there, pushing to get work, but success eluded many of them. There is a belief that if you have talent, study, go to every audition, send out pictures and résumés, and pursue your dream with a fervor, you'll make it. And there's another notion that if you're really talented, someone will somehow "discover" you. This book was written out of the realization that these beliefs aren't completely true. Show business is a business. And like any business, it must be approached with a strategy, game plan, and the proper artillery. There are specific ways to achieve what you dream about. This book was written for the actor who is ready and willing to work. It's a resource book of facts, ideas, and suggestions.

The book begins with an in-depth discussion of headshots. Headshots are one of the main promotional tools available to an actor. But before you even think of calling a photographer, you must have a firm understanding of what specific "type" you are. You must also know how you're planning to market yourself. I discuss type in chapters 1 and 6. Marketing is discussed in chapter 6, "Personal

Marketing." Without a thorough understanding of marketing, there's a good chance that your headshot, although personally flattering, might not be totally effective.

While researching this book, I learned that there's more to a mailing campaign than just sending out headshots and postcards. Actors must be very specific as to who they target, why, and how. Initial cover letters must be well thought out. Follow-up mailings must be thorough and also well planned. In chapter 5, I suggest ways to make every single mailing effective. The idea is to get your reader's attention and interest immediately, and then to keep it.

Throughout the book I look at the many ways actors can promote themselves, from making videotapes to voice-over demos, to producing one-person shows to independent films. I think you'll discover as you go through the book that there's a great deal you can do for yourself besides sitting home waiting for the phone to ring.

I think that chapter 13, "Networking," will be as eye-opening for you as it was for me. While researching this subject, I realized that I never really knew the first thing about effective networking. One lesson I learned is that it's a lot more than a friendly hello and handshake at a party. Here, too, strategy, commitment, and perseverance are everything. And don't for one minute underestimate the importance of networking in show business. It's one of the major ways that the business is run. If you walk away from this book with nothing but a thorough understanding of how to effectively network in show business, I think you'll have achieved a great deal.

Although I interviewed over one hundred people for the book, I included only fifty-five of the most informative interviews. Agents, casting directors, managers, photographers, voice-over specialists, videographers, and more, are all represented. I asked questions that I felt every actor would want answered. The section on casting directors (chapter 28) is by far the largest one in the book. I was very fortunate in getting interviews with some of the most powerful (and constantly working) casting directors in the business. I am extremely grateful for their willingness to share what I feel is invaluable information. I think you'll find the answers to such questions as, What do you look for at an audition (and interview)? or, What is the one thing that really ticks you off about actors? or, If you had one piece of advice to offer actors about their careers what would it be? particularly illuminating. I know I did.

The task of getting casting directors, agents, producers, and directors to know who you are is not easy. Turning a talented, struggling actor into a steadily working one can be accomplished with perseverance, tact, and know-how. That's what this book is about. It's written for the actor who just got off the bus as well as for the seasoned professional.

I sincerely wish you the best in your attempts to meet your goals and realize your dreams. That's why I wrote this book.

GLENN ALTERMAN

# Headshots: Your Calling Card

**O**ne of the most important marketing tools that actors have is the headshot. For that reason, several chapters of the book cover this topic. The headshot creates the first impression that casting directors, directors, and producers have of you. Hopefully your headshot expresses the image that you're trying to create for yourself. Quite often it determines the kind of auditions and work you'll be getting. It is your calling card and an important marketing tool.

### What You See Is What You Get

Casting directors get hundreds of pictures each week. Making sure that yours stands out from the rest is very important. This eight-by-ten-inch black-and-white photo is one of the most important ingredients in your self-promotion package. But it must, and I can't stress this enough, look like you: not the you that only exists in your imagination, not the you that's been so retouched that not one slight imperfection shows, and not the you that some photographer has lit so dramatically that all we see now are teeth and eyes, but the best *you* you can be! Later on, when you've read the interviews with the casting directors and talent agents, you'll learn just how important they feel this is. There is nothing more embarrassing than the look on the casting director's face when you enter her office, she looks up, and you can tell that she doesn't feel you resemble your photo in the least. Disappointment and rejection are in the wings. You're starting that interview/audition with several points off—an unnecessary handicap. The photo must look like you! Something else to keep in mind is the attitude of your picture. A pose that's too dramatic, too artsy, or too aloof will leave the casting director uninterested. What you want is a friendly, open, interesting shot. Your shoulders should be relaxed, your smile not forced. Be a strong participant in your photo session. Make sure the photographer and you are in total agreement as to what type you are, how you're marketing yourself, and what it is you're trying to say with your headshot.

### Types of Headshots

*The commercial headshot,* used for all commercial auditions, should be a photo of you smiling, preferably with teeth visible. Here's your chance to express your warmth and enthusiasm. Your photo should be saying, Hi, I'm here and I'm confident. Your smile should express friendliness. Your eyes, which is where most casting directors say they look first, should be warm, intelligent, and eager, *but definitely not desperate!*

*Your theatrical or "legit" headshot* should be a bit more dramatic, more relaxed. This is the photo used for submissions to theater, TV, and film. There's no need to do a hard sell here. As one photographer said, "I like the actors to just be for these photos. Let me catch them." The feeling that you should be expressing in this photo is that you're comfortable with yourself. The casting directors and talent agents that I interviewed said they look for "aliveness, intelligence—especially in the eyes."

*The soap headshot* might be a smart investment if you're attractive, sexy, somewhat glamorous, or romantic looking (or can be). It's not really necessary, however, to have a soap shot. You can always use your theatrical (legit) photo for soaps. If you're in doubt as to what you should do, speak to your agent or a casting director about it.

*The portrait style headshot* (a three-quarter, body shot) has become increasingly popular in the last few years. Since more of the body is shown in these photos, some casting directors prefer them because they get a better sense of how the actor will look in person. The size of people's heads are sometimes quite different from the size and shape of their bodies. These photographs have a wide white border with a thin black line inside.

### Selecting a Photographer

Many photographers place ads in *Backstage* and *Drama-Logue,* but I feel the best way to find a photographer is the same way you might find a doctor or lawyer, through recommendation. I advise asking around. Ask other actors in your acting class or at auditions. Ask casting directors and agents you are in contact with who they recommend. Look at other actors' headshots. If one really impresses you, find out who the photographer was. Then ask the actor some of the following pertinent questions:

- Were you comfortable during the shoot?
- Did you feel rushed?
- Did you enjoy the shoot?
- Did you feel that you collaborated well with the photographer or did he just give orders that you felt obliged to follow?
- Were you relaxed at the session?
- How much time did the photographer allow for the sitting?
- How much did he charge (rates can change)?

After you've gathered five to eight names of photographers, call them and set up appointments to meet with them and look at their portfolios. Photographers fees for headshots range from about $150 to $650 (and higher). Price, by the way, should be only one factor in your decision making. Getting the cheapest deal or having your headshot taken by the most "in" photographer is not the way to select a photographer. The most important consideration is how you feel with the photographer, the "vibe."

Do you feel relaxed/comfortable? Does the photographer rush the initial interview? Does he answer all your questions satisfactorily? Find out the specific financial terms of the photo shoot. The following are some questions you should keep in mind:

- How many prints will I get for the fee?
- If I want extra prints how much will they cost?
- Does retouching/airbrushing cost extra?
- How much time do you allow for a photo session?
- Are negatives of my photos included in the price?
- How long after the session will I have to wait for my photos?
- Do you shoot outdoors?
- If I have to cancel, how much advance notice must I give to avoid being charged?

Don't be shy about asking questions. If a photographer is reluctant to answer some of your questions or you feel that he is hiding something—trust your instincts as to whether or not you should work with him.

### Looking at Portfolios

At your interview with the photographer, she should show you her portfolio. If for any reason she cannot show it to you then, arrange for a time when she can. Never book a session with any photographer unless you've seen her work! When looking at the photographer's portfolio, keep in mind the following questions:

#### The Lighting
- Does the lighting have a natural look?
- Is it too dramatic?
- Do the actors' features seem washed out?
- Do the actors' skin tones seem realistic?
- Does the lighting show the contours of the actors' faces?
- Can you tell by the lighting if the actors are blonds, brunets, or redheads?
- Does the photographer use backlighting?
- Does the lighting call too much attention to itself?

#### Look at the Actors
- Do they seem relaxed?
- If you were a casting director/agent looking at these photos, what would you think?

- Do you feel that the photographer got these actors to express something about themselves to you?
- Is there a sameness to all the photos?
- Do you feel this photographer works just as well with women as with men?
- Do you like the quality of this photographer's work?
- Does it seem cheaply done? Rushed?
- What's your overall feeling about the photos?

### Preparing for the Shoot

A good photographic shoot, like a good audition, will go best if you prepare well in advance. Don't wait for the last minute to make decisions. After you've selected the photographer and picked the date, you should consider the following in preparation for the shoot.

### Knowing Your Type and How to Dress

One very important aspect of your being able to market yourself well is to know your "type." What type are you? Mom? Upscale? Exec? All-American? Whatever type you are, dress accordingly, but don't go overboard. Think *wardrobe* not *costume.* Type is determined first by your physical appearance (height, weight, face, etc.). Your personality and acting ability also add into the equation. Can you convince America in thirty seconds that you are a mom and that that's your baby? Can you convince people that you're the CEO of that company? The more you know how to market your type, the more successful you'll be, especially in TV commercials (and print work). Types such as college kid, young mom, executive, model, and mom and pop are just a few of the classifications used to cast commercials. Look at magazine ads and see how many different types you can find. Watch TV and notice the types used in commercials. Try to see which commercials you'd be right for. Naturally this does not mean that this type is all you are. You are a living, breathing, multitalented actor with many levels and dimensions to your talent. Some actors take typecasting too personally. They feel that they are more than just a nerd or a mom. And they're right. But remember, it's just a business. Play the game and you may win. Be a maverick and you probably won't. You may also want to check with casting directors and agents that you know to ask their opinions on what type you are and how you should be marketing yourself.

Identifying costume symbols such as pins, props, jewelry, or hats should be avoided. There is nothing wrong, however, in shooting a couple of shots wearing prop glasses (as long as that works for your type).

### Tips for Women: Makeup and Hair

Women should always wear makeup at a photographic shoot. Whether you do your own makeup or hire someone else depends on how confident you feel about it. For some actresses, just knowing that a professional stylist will take care of their makeup for them frees them up to deal with other aspects of the shoot. In either case, your makeup should be used just to enhance, not to hide or cover up. Always remember that your photo should look like the person who will be walking into the casting director's/agent's office. You should look like you at your best. You want your natural skin tones to show. And always remember when applying makeup that the photos are in black and white. If your makeup is too dramatic, it can make you look older or less attractive. In choosing lipstick colors, think of how the shade will contrast with your skin.

When considering hairstyles for headshots, you shouldn't choose a style that is too trendy. Hopefully, you'll be able to use the photo for a few years. Besides, the photo shouldn't be just about hair. "Big hair" probably will take up too much focus.

### Tips for Men: Makeup and Hair

One word to keep in mind—moderation. Many actors shave right before the shoot. It's been suggested that you shouldn't shave for a day or so before the shoot so that you'll get an especially good shave the day of the shoot. Also, use a light amount of makeup for the session. Without makeup, men's skin tends to look too washed out. As far as hairstyles—don't go overboard. As one photographer said, "Don't Elvis it up!" Not too much mousse or cream; it will make your hair greasy-looking on film.

## At the Photo Shoot

Once the session gets underway, remember the following:

- Relax.
- You never want to seem too posed. Some feeling should always be coming from inside. Some actors actually give themselves acting tasks to keep themselves from becoming too self-conscious.
- You've heard it before, but here it is again: *Think of the camera as your friend (a close friend, an intimate friend!).*
- Legit/theater headshot and the portrait headshot: The feeling behind the photo should be one of confidence. What they're looking for is someone intelligent, interesting, exciting. Try not to make it too posed. Feel free to be spontaneous. Be expressive, courageous.
- Commercial headshot: A smile. A real smile that emanates from within. A smile that has teeth but isn't too toothy. It should be an open, enthusiastic smile. A smile that at it's core stands for only one word—Yes!
- Soap headshot: One word—SEX. But not too trashy. Playful, romantic, secretive, and alluring.

# Now That the Photo Session Is Over, What Next?

**O**nce the shoot is complete, the first challenge is to pick your headshot from the contact sheet. When selecting which photo to use, keep one thing in mind: Your vote counts the most! After you've made your initial selections, show the contact sheet to actor friends, casting directors, and agents whose opinions you trust. After everyone has made his or her selections (using either different colored pencils or initialing), look at the contact sheet again—*you* have the final vote. Remember, this is your calling card, this photo represents you. Try to be subjective. Look at the photo as if it were not you, but someone you didn't know. What do you think of that person in the photo? Do you like him or her? Would you want to know him or her? What type is he or she? For some actors being able to detach themselves and select photos can be difficult. If that's a problem for you, then I suggest you simply go along with the person whose opinion you trust the most.

### Retouching

Be careful when it comes to retouching, the tendency is to overdo it. Yes, you may remove that blemish that appeared somehow on the day of the shoot. But if it's permanent, don't get rid of it. It's part of you. If you like, you may lighten those dark, unflattering circles under your eyes that somehow appeared in the photograph but aren't part of you. If you wish, you can soften some of those lines in your face that don't normally appear but were somehow frozen in the photo. Retouching is a team effort. Each change should be carefully discussed with the photographer or the retoucher.

### Reproductions

After you've received your prints back, they've been retouched, and you're happy with them, there is one last thing to do: get reproductions. It would seem a shame to put all that energy into your headshot and then make inferior reproductions. Here are some things to keep in mind when selecting a studio or lab to make the reproductions:

- Always look at the studio's headshot book.
- Are you pleased with the type of work they do?
- Do you like the paper they use?
- Do they answer all your questions satisfactorily?
- Do they provide test shots for you to look at (before running off the reproductions)? Do they charge extra for this service?
- Always remember that reproductions increase the contrast of your original photo. In some cases this may be flattering, but in others it can be too dramatic or unflattering.
- When selecting from the test shots, always choose the photo that is the most like your original.

### The Do's and Don'ts of Mailings

I will briefly touch on some issues to be aware of when doing your mailings. For further, in-depth information about mailings, see chapter 5.

- Always mail your photos in manilla envelopes with cardboard inserts.
- On the envelope, print the words "DO NOT BEND." The post office is famous for mangling mailers.
- Always include a cover letter with your mailings. Included in this brief note should be a short self-introduction. Mention

how you came to write to them (a friend, relative, business acquaintance, etc.).

- *Always* request an appointment. What's the point of the mailing if it's not to get to meet them in person? Tell them you'll call in a week or so. Then be sure to call them in a week or so! (More likely than not, you won't get through, but sometimes you just might, especially if they saw something in your photo or in your note that interested them.)
- If you do get through, be brief, cordial, and professional. Don't get chatty or too familiar.
- If you have a video or audiotape, mention it in your cover letter. Tell them that you'd like to have them look at it at their convenience.
- Don't write your note by hand if you have illegible handwriting, type it.
- Don't guess the spelling of the name of the person to whom you are writing. Make sure it is correct. Look it up somewhere or make a phone call to find out.
- Know the sex of the person to whom you're writing. Even names like Glenn or Michael may belong to a woman.
- When writing to women, it's always safer to use "Ms." rather than "Mrs." or "Miss."
- If, when you call a couple of weeks later, you don't get through, wait a few days and then send a postcard politely requesting an appointment.

### Picture Postcards

Aside from headshots, you'll need a supply of picture postcards that you can get from the reproduction studio when you have your headshots made. As with your headshot, you should list your name, union affiliations, and contact numbers under the photo on the front of the card. Most often, actors select their commercial headshot for the postcard, too. Whichever photo you use, it should be friendly, open, and able to capture the eye of the receiver. Many actors use these postcards incorrectly. (Agents and casting directors discuss the use of postcards in chapters 18 and 28.)

Postcards are best used to inform casting directors and agents about progress in your career, to thank them for a job they recently hired you for, or sometimes may be included in the envelope with fliers for shows you're currently performing in. I know of a few actors who mail their postcards in envelopes, paying the regular mail rate rather than the postcard rate. Their thinking is that in an envelope a postcard will be individually looked at by the casting director (rather than be just one of hundreds received each week). It's up to you and your budget.

If you're about to appear on a soap or in a movie, use the postcard to announce your news. Like many other good things, postcards can be abused. They should not be sent too often. If you feel you want to, using them once a month just to say "hello" is fine. More than that is a waste of time, energy, and postage.

# CHAPTER 3

# *Interviews*
## *with Photographers and*
## *Reproduction Studio Owners*

### The Photographers

ARTHUR COHEN (**AC**) has been a photographer in New York City for about fourteen years. He has photographed many celebrities but prefers to keep his client list private. He also works for a number of different magazines, shoots album covers, and does photo editorials.

JINSEY DAUK (**JD**) has her work represented in most casts of Broadway shows today. She has been a celebrity photographer for many years. She shot all the new models at such agencies as Ford and Elite for several years. Her specialty is that she "brings naturalism" to headshots by not using a flash in her photo sessions.

KONSTANTIN (**K**) has been a photographer for twenty-six years. He has photographed President Nixon, Mayor Ed Koch (of New York City), and all the TV news anchorpeople whose photos are currently on display at bus stops in New York City.

NICK GRANITO (**NG**) has been in the business for over twenty-one years. He has photographed such stars as Wesley Snipes and Christian Slater.

BETH KUKUCK (**BK**) has been a photographer for over sixteen years. She prefers to use natural lighting and does a great deal of location work (along with in-house work). One of the things she's well known for is taking her clients to exciting, hidden locations to be photographed.

---

**What would you say are the most common mistakes actors make at a photo session?**

**AC:** The most common mistake is the one they make before the photo session: their marketing plans, their types. Not knowing how to market themselves is major. If you don't know what type you are, then you can't make the right decisions as to what to wear, your hair, your look, etc. Other mistakes include coming in for a shooting after getting a bad haircut, bringing the wrong clothes, or getting headshots before you're ready.

**JD:** The thing that bothers me the most is when I feel the actors don't seem to care. Perhaps they got the session as a gift or whatever. What I'll feel is that there is no collaboration with me. Perhaps they're just feeling insecure or cut off emotionally, but the energy is dead. It makes my job very hard.

**K:** It's very simple. They are insecure and they don't know themselves well enough. Work on yourself. Be confident. Everyone is nervous, even the biggest stars. Just don't show it. Also, try not to come to be photographed with a tan.

**NG:** They don't know what they want out of the session. Quite often they don't know what type they are. Another thing, they make their headshot session too important. A headshot is just a calling card, it's not a résumé. The bottom line is if you're working a lot you'll never need a headshot again. Too many actors watch themselves during the shoot, don't trust the photographer, and just don't have fun.

**BK:** Most actors assume that the shots they want, the ones that'll be chosen for their headshot, will be taken during the first roll of film. The first roll of film should be just for a warm-up. The first roll usually is a little stiff, no matter how comfortable you are in front of the camera. People tend to tense their necks a little bit to get a certain look. This tensing creates lines in the neck (which I can take out in the darkroom).

**What criteria do you feel actors should use when selecting a photographer?**

**AC:** You should ask yourself, Do you like this photographer's style? Do you like the photographer? Are you comfortable in the studio? Does the photographer come highly recommended? Bottom line—it should be a visceral, gut feeling that this photographer is right for you.

**JD:** They have to see a warmth in the photographer's pictures when they're looking at his or her portfolio. They should, most importantly, feel some kind of connection with the photographer.

**K:** They should never make an appointment for a session just based on an ad in the newspaper or how well someone from a studio talks to them on the phone. Meet the photographer, see the studio, see any additional work the photographer can show you. By meeting the photographer in person you'll be able to determine if you'll work well with him.

**NG:** They should look at the photographer's portfolio. They should select five photographers in their price range, then interview them. The *main thing*: they should feel comfortable with the photographer. When looking at his book, ask yourself how technically proficient is he? Is the photographer good with your type? Does the photographer only shoot good-looking people? Can he shoot character people? Not that many photographers, you'll find, work equally well with men and women.

**BK:** How comfortable they are, and how competent the photographer seems. The price also is a consideration for many actors. If a photographer is too expensive for the actor's budget, the actor will look somewhere else.

### How can actors prepare for a shoot?

**AC:** Again, marketing is the best way you can prepare. Be in as good a shape as you can be. Know who you are and what it is that makes you unique.

**JD:** Bringing your own music can be of some help. Bring something that relaxes you, that can get you ready to play. If you're nervous, *that's good!* We can use that energy. Iron your clothes. Make sure your nails are clean and even in length.

**K:** That is almost totally unnecessary. If they have a good connection with the photographer then it's the photographer's job to make them totally at ease.

**NG:** Just come in with the mind-set that you'll have fun and trust the photographer. Bring more clothes than less, so that the photographer will have a choice. I believe women should do their own hair. Make sure your hair is clean and dry (unless it looks better a few days after it's washed). I don't feel a hairdresser should do your hair for a shoot. Sometimes exercise helps before you come in. Just feel good about yourself the day of the shoot. Be focused, know what you want from the session. Get lots of rest, drink lots of water.

**BK:** Practice in the mirror. Discover what angles and what looks you like best. Go through your wardrobe, find things that you're most comfortable in.

### What type and how much wardrobe do you recommend actors bring to the shoot?

**AC:** I like to do four or five really good changes. They should be clothes you love and are really comfortable in. The clothes should reflect both your type and personality.

**JD:** I usually feel that you should bring eleven or twelve things and then when you get here we can go through the clothes together. More is better than less. Clothes should direct all the attention to your face. Solid colored things work best. Bright white doesn't, black does. Textures are wonderful. The most effective headshots are where the clothes are secondary and we're not aware of what you're wearing.

**K:** From three to six changes for both actors and actresses. If the actor is a clean-cut, all-American type, he should definitely bring a white shirt; not gray, not blue, not any other color. Also a tie and a jacket, for going up for parts like a spokesperson, attorney, whatever. If you're not the clean-cut type and don't normally wear jackets and ties, don't bring them. Only bring clothes that you feel comfortable in. Ladies who are all-American should bring a white blouse, a blazer, for that corporate executive look. Never bring clothes that are striped or heavily designed. As I mentioned, I'm a photographer that likes white (many photographers don't), as well as black. Those actors who are not all-American types should bring some wardrobe that would project the exact parts they'd like to play. Cast yourselves. Use the studio as a starting off point to project yourself into those roles you've always wanted. If you feel very good in a denim jacket with the collar rolled up, a leather jacket, jeans, sport shirts, turtlenecks, bring them. On the other hand, if you're an actor who feels great in tails and a tuxedo, bring them. You have to draw the picture for the casting people.

**NG:** Most actors don't know, they just see in colors. Headshots are shot in black and white. I tell actors to bring several changes, I edit their clothes when they come over. I like black a lot. The clothes should express who you are. Generally they show a little more skin for soaps or film.

**BK:** Anything but white. White tends to be the main focus of a photograph. If a woman has big arms, or arms that she doesn't want to be so noticeable in a photograph, she shouldn't wear something short sleeved. I don't have any particular suggestions for a look, just something that they're comfortable in. Bring very little wardrobe to the shoot. For those people that bring a lot of clothing, I find that we rarely get through three or four different outfits. Not too much wardrobe is better.

**Any cosmetic tips for men and women at a shoot?**

**AC:** Don't have a heavy tan or you'll photograph muddy. Make sure your hair is exactly the right length and color before the shoot. At some times of the year some people's skin is drier and flakier—don't shoot then (unless you've taken care of it with humidifiers and moisturizers). If your hair is damaged in the summer, make sure to take care of that before the session. I like people to be close to their ideal weight. If you're going to have any cosmetic dental work, make sure you're comfortable with how it feels before you set up a photo session.

**JD:** The rule of thumb here is whatever you see in the mirror is exactly what you're going to get. Women should come to the shoot with their hair and makeup already done. They can do last-minute stuff right before the shoot. Men—wear no makeup. Blending makeup is very important, otherwise you'll look like a Fellini clown on film. Women should use two powder puffs to blend foundation, blush, and powder together.

**K:** I do my own makeup at my shoots. I know my studio, my lights, so who could do it better? Being able to work with an actor's bone structure to make her more attractive is really the point here.

**NG:** I don't like makeup on men, I think it makes them too feminine, too young looking. I take care of frizzy hair here. With women, the makeup is very important. I have powder and retouch here. Makeup enhances a woman's photo.

**BK:** On the day of the shoot, be aware of lines under your eyes, if your eyes have gotten puffy. If you notice these things, you should know how to cover them cosmetically. Be real light on the jewelry. The basic rule is don't let any other part of you speak louder than your face.

**How often do you feel actors should get new headshots?**

**AC:** Not until you've changed substantially from your last headshot.

**JD:** Probably every eight years. Unless the actor has changed a lot. If he's lost a lot of weight, changed his hair, then perhaps sooner.

**K:** Only when they really feel they have changed a lot, or if they've changed something about themselves. If the actress has cut her hair, become a blonde, whatever. If the guy had long hair and now cut it short—it's time.

**NG:** If they're working, very rarely. If the headshot is working for you, go with it until someone says get another shot. Usually women go more than men. A woman usually gets new shots every two years; a guy every four or five years.

**BK:** I've always thought if I was an actor I'd get them done every six months or so. That's why I feel that headshots should be affordable. I have a friend that does get new headshots every six months. Her look changes every six months. But for the average actor, it really depends on her particular needs and how often her look changes.

**What should actors be thinking during the shoot? Is there something that they can focus on to help make their pictures look more alive?**

**AC:** I work very easy when I shoot, very conversational. If they want some more dramatic shots, I'll ask them to run a little monologue in their brain. I'm not a real "coacher," I'm more relaxed in the way I work.

**JD:** It's not an acting exercise. You have to be willing to allow the photographer to direct you. The more you can play into his or her directions, relax and just go with the moment, the better your pictures will come out. Mainly we aim for spontaneity in each picture. Aliveness. I usually tell my clients to close their eyes and think about something funny. When they open their eyes, I start shooting. Remember, the casting director wants to feel the life, the spirit, come through in the photo.

**K:** Nothing. It's like being on a movie set where the director tells you what to do. The photographer should be able to direct the actor through the poses. The actor just has to show up and be as open as he or she can. Background music should not be necessary.

**NG:** You should focus on just feeling comfortable. It's up to the photographer to help make you feel secure enough so that you can put out the warmth and emotion that's needed for the shot.

**BK:** You should focus on your eyes and what you want to say with your eyes. Whether it be surprise or seduction or whatever look you want to have. Be as comfortable as you can. I quite often ask people to bring something that they might want to hold onto while they're shooting (since I usually don't include the hands). It can be anything from a pen to a key chain. It should be something that they can put their tension into. I always provide music (usually Joni Mitchell), but actors can bring whatever music they'd like to hear. Taking breaks is useful. Usually every half a roll or so we'll take a short break. No matter how aware you are or how alive you are, after a couple of frames the energy in the eyes starts to die. Step back, take a breather, a glass of water. I prefer to do location work because it distracts people. I've found that people are more comfortable outdoors and on location. I know some great locations.

**Specifically regarding your studio: What is included in a session? How much do you charge? How many pictures are taken?**

**AC:** Two unretouched eight-by-tens, four rolls of film (144 shots). I also do Polaroid previews. I charge $525 plus tax for a session. (If you need a stylist, it's $145 more.)

**JD:** I charge $495 for three rolls (each roll has thirty-six exposures).

**K:** I cover everything that's necessary within seventy-two shots. That means commercial, three-quarter shots, dramatic, semidramatic, and an all-around shot. They get two eight-by-ten enlargements of their choice. Presently, I charge $225 for my session.

**NG:** You get two eight-by-tens, 180 shots, the negatives, and one retouched print. I charge $235.

**BK:** I charge $250 for three rolls. You get the processed contact sheets with an eight-by-ten for each roll (thirty-six pictures per roll).

### How much time does each session take?

**AC:** I allow four hours, but generally my male sessions are two hours, my female sessions are three.

**JD:** I allow two hours for each session. Since I don't use flash, there is no lost time (or energy) to my sessions.

**K:** Never more than an hour.

**NG:** Two-and-a-half to three hours.

**BK:** Anywhere from one to four hours. The average is a couple of hours.

### How much in advance do you need to book for a session?

**AC:** Right now it's six weeks, but typically it's two months in advance.

**JD:** It depends. Anywhere from two weeks to a month.

**K:** A few days in advance.

**NG:** Usually a week.

**BK:** About two weeks.

### The Photo Reproduction Studio Owners

CARL CANIZARES (**CC**) is the owner of Ideal Photos, which has been in the business for thirty-three years.

CAMERON STEWART (**CS**) is the owner of Reproductions. He's been in the photographic field for nineteen years and at Reproductions for five.

### In selecting a photo reproduction studio, what things should an actor look for?

**CC:** One of the best things is recommendation. Ask other actors who they use. They should look around and see how the studio looks. They should look for samples of past work displayed on the walls and ask to see the sample book of past customers' photos. The initial contact with the salesperson is very important. As far as questions are concerned, I feel that any question you have regarding your photo is appropriate. Don't be shy. One question to ask is, If you don't like your photos will the lab redo them? If you want your photos airbrushed or retouched, make sure you're clear about exactly what you want. Just so you know, retouching is done on the eight-by-ten negative. It's good for things like softening under the eyes. Airbrushing is done on the original photograph. Say an actress has a lot of frizzy hair in the photo, we can airbrush or erase some of it away. Airbrushing is also used for big bags under the eyes. I usually advise people not to remove things from the photo that are part of you. You don't want to look too different from your photo.

Before continuing my answer to your question, I'd like your readers to know just how photo reproductions are done. There are two ways of reproducing photos. First is projection enlargements. These cost about $1.20 apiece. If you order a hundred of these projection enlargement pieces, you're talking about $120. Obviously, for that money it's the top-quality work. The second way is contact reproduction, meaning "same-size negative, same-size print." The cost here is 40¢ a print or $40 for a hundred photos. This is the way that most actors have their headshots reproduced.

**CS:** Quality, service, and a willingness of the lab to work with them and help them. Actors are purchasing something that is out of their normal field. Pictures are, in a sense, an advertising piece. They should ask the photographer they're working with to suggest a reproduction lab. That is one of the best ways I know of to find a lab. Since they've hired the photographer as a technical professional, they should trust his advice. Also, in the theatrical community there is a tremendous amount of word of mouth going around. That's another good way to find a reproduction lab.

### What are the most common problems actors make when bringing in their photos?

**CC:** Something I'd like to mention here is to be careful of labs that rip actors off. An actor recently came in with a beautiful print and asked if he had to "prepare the photo." I had no idea what he meant by "prepare." He told me he went to another lab and was told that it would be $25 to prepare the photo. What?! This was an obvious rip-off and I hear quite a few studios are now doing it! As far as I know, there is no such thing as "preparing" a photo. Be careful. Let the buyer beware.

As to your question, actors expect the reproductions to look exactly like the original. That's impossible. There's usually about a 10 percent difference in quality.

**CS:** I think that the most important thing for actors to realize is that this is a business. Many actors come in and go at this in sort of a half-hearted sense. To really succeed in any business venture is to really go for it! Consequently we have actors come in and buy like fifty copies of their photos, something like that. In a sense, they're wasting their money. Fifty copies aren't going to get you very far. You need to work with extensive mailings, get your name out there. In order to do that, you need to work with a greater volume of pictures, which also consequently goes to a lower per unit value. Actually, I'd make more money if every actor came in through the door and ordered only fifty copies. Look at it as an investment in copies as an advertising venture in a business.

**What should actors expect and not expect from reproductions?**

**CC:** They should expect a good quality photo similar to the original. They should also expect good service and work done relatively inexpensively. Sometimes photos are too dramatic, lightingwise. These photos tend to look more unlike the originals than those with less-dramatic lighting.

**CS:** Actors must be prepared for the subtle differences between their original and the reproduction copies. Sometimes actors expect an exact match.

**Any suggestions you have regarding eight-by-tens and postcards?**

**CC:** One problem I've noticed is when actors shoot outdoors with photographers who aren't too savvy about lighting. Foolishly, the photographer shoots them directly under the sun at twelve o'clock. These photos give the actor a look of bags under the eyes—not good. When you reproduce something like that, the shadows get even darker. Also, always use the originals for your reproductions, not a second-generation photo.

Most actors tend to use their headshot photos for their postcards. Don't get too many eight-by-tens at once. Get what you need for a while, a few months to a year. I once had someone order 3,500 eight-by-tens. Don't ask me why. I'm sure he still has plenty and that was years ago. Don't forget, every few years you'll probably get a new one.

Also, try to match the print for your name to the type of photo and your personality. It may look strange, say, for a lady with a pretty face to have strong block print with her photo. Or a macho guy using delicate script lettering. It works against the look, doesn't carry the photo.

**CS:** You must scrutinize the original photo before giving it to a lab. Too often, actors will select a photo without looking at the photo's details. Then, after you've made up a hundred copies, you realize that there are little distracting things that you've never considered. Look carefully at those atmospheric features in the background. Something might be more distracting than you realize.

**Any other photo items actors can use for self-promotion?**

**CC:** We also make business cards for actors with their photos on them. Some actors find these cards effective and quite compact. They have them in their wallets, and if they meet someone in the business at a social function they can hand it to them right there. It's a great networking tool, less cumbersome than an eight-by-ten. Our business is about 80 percent eight-by-tens, 18 percent postcards, and only about 2 percent business cards.

**CS:** Photo reproductions are also used for voice-over cassette covers and opening announcements for plays and nightclub acts. One thing I always suggest is, know your audience. That is, know who you're targeting and find the best tool, be it a photo or whatever, to get their attention.

# Résumés

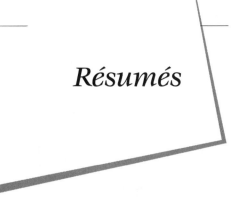

**A**n actor's résumé is quite different than a business résumé, both in content and format. Knowing what and what not to put on the résumé is very important. The résumé should be professional looking and to the point. Simply put, you should list whatever experience (professional or showcase) you've had, who you've trained with and where. The résumé should never be handwritten. Have it typed professionally and check it carefully for typos.

The résumé is *attached* to the back of your picture. I emphasize the word "attached" because so often résumés are poorly attached and fall off, leaving your picture stranded. When the casting director/agent turns your picture over, guess what? There's nothing there. Into the garbage can your picture goes. To avoid this, carefully staple or glue the photo to the back of your résumé. Some actors actually have their résumés copied directly onto the back of their photos. There's certainly no chance of it ever getting lost that way. No matter what, make sure that your résumé fits properly on the picture. If it's too big, the edges will get torn or curled.

### What to Include on Your Résumé

All the casting directors that I interviewed were very clear about what they want to see on a résumé. They want to know "the truth, the whole truth, and nothing. . . ."

But if your experience is limited, is it okay to "fudge" a bit? Let me just say that many actors do. Not big lies, but little ones. It's certainly not too bright to claim you've played the Phantom in *The Phantom of the Opera* on Broadway if you haven't. Some casting directors (see chapter 28) are immediately turned off if they detect even a little lie. A major pet peeve of many casting directors is misspellings. The information should be listed by category (not randomly). Some casting directors have suggested using an off-white color paper (such as beige) because it cuts down on the glare from harsh office lights. This may be an unnecessary expense. It's up to you.

### The Format and Order of Information

Your résumé should only be one page long. It should be neatly printed, well organized, and well typed. The following information should appear exactly the same on either a New York résumé or a Los Angeles résumé:

#### The Heading

- First of all, your name should be at the top. It should be in a different font or style from the rest of the text below.
- If you belong to any performing unions, you should list them directly below your name.
- A few spaces down, on the left-hand side of the page, you should list a telephone number where you can be reached, a beeper number, or an answering service number. Since you really never know where your résumé will end up, it's suggested that you don't list your home phone number.
- On the right-hand side of the page, directly across from your telephone number, list your height.
- Below your height, list your weight; below that, your hair color; below that, the color of your eyes.
- If you are a singer or dancer, include the pertinent information (voice type and what type of dancing you do).

## Example of the Heading on Top of an Actor's Résumé

### JOE ACTOR
(SAG AFTRA AEA)

| | |
|---|---|
| Beeper: (212) 769-2247 | Height: 6'1" |
| Answering Machine: (212) 967-5540 | Weight: 182 |
| Diane Arnsly Talent Agency | Hair: Brown |
| Agent's Phone: (212) 655-8876 | Eyes: Hazel |

### The Body of the Résumé

The main difference between the New York résumé and the Los Angeles résumé is the emphasis on certain credits. In Los Angeles, which is mostly a movie and TV town, casting directors want to know what films and episodic TV work you've done. In New York City (and Chicago), they are more interested in what theater work you've done and who you've trained with.

### The New York Résumé

#### Order of Necessary Information

- *Theater credits* are usually listed first. Name the play, your role, and the theater. Under the theater category you should list whether you worked on Broadway, off Broadway, or in regional theater. Some actors list the directors with whom they've worked (especially if they're well known).
- Next list any *film credits* you have. Include each film's title and the role you played (whether it was a leading role, featured role, or supporting role).
- Beneath this category you should list any *television credits* you have, including the show's title and the character's name.
- In the *commercial* category, which is next, it is not necessary to list all the TV and radio spots that you've done. All they need to know is whether you've done on-camera and/or voice-over work and whether or not you have a reel. Most people usually state "list available upon request."
- *Training* should include the type of training you received

(acting, voice, speech, dance), and the teacher's name and/
or school.
- List any *special skills* that you have, such as marathon runner,
  yoga instructor, and/or any language that you speak fluently.

### Example of the New York Résumé

## LAURENCE APPLETON

Service: (212) 769- 2320                           Height: 6'1"
Agent: Steven Drucker Talent                       Weight: 175
Agent's Phone Number: (212) 777-6687               Hair: Brown
                                                   Eyes: Hazel

| THEATRE | | | |
|---|---|---|---|
| Off-Broadway | *As Is* | Saul | Circle Rep. |
| | *My Life* | Paul | Soho Rep. |
| Regional | *Men in White* | Pete | George St. Playhouse |
| | | | (East Brunswick, New Jersey) |
| | *The Zoo Story* | Jerry | Yale Rep. Theater |
| | | | |
| TELEVISION | *Loving* | Steve | ABC-TV *(recurring)* |

COMMERCIALS    Have done on-camera principals—over 45 national
               network and regional spots (tape available upon request)

TRAINING       Acting: Scene Study with Uta Hagen (H.B. Studio)
               Voice: Ed Dixon
               Speech: Merilee Nolan

SPECIAL SKILLS  Yoga instructor, marathon runner, speak French

### The Los Angeles Résumé

### Order of Necessary Information

The main difference between the résumé of the actor seeking work
in Los Angeles as compared to New York City is placement of

categories. (For a definition of each category, see the New York Résumé: Order of Necessary Information, above.)

- *Film* experience should be listed first.
- *Television* is next.
- *Commercials* ("list available upon request").
- *Theater* is listed below that.
- *Training* is next.
- *Special skills* are listed last.

### Example of the Los Angeles Résumé

## INA SMALL

Service: (213) 769-7789

| Height: 5'5" | Weight: 140 |
|---|---|
| Hair: Red | Eyes: Blue |

**FILM**

| *Queen of the Valley* | Roma (lead) | Red Eye Films |
|---|---|---|

**TELEVISION**

| *Murphy Brown* | Ann Leard (guest star) | CBS-TV |
|---|---|---|
| *Seaquest* | Mila (featured role) | NBC-TV |

**THEATRE**

| *Barefoot in the Park* | Corie | Weathervane Theater |
|---|---|---|
| *Promises, Promises* | Fran Kubelik | Hempstead Playhouse |

COMMERCIALS    On-camera principals—national network spots (list available on request)

TRAINING    Acting: Terry Schreiber (3 years), Larry Moss (2 years)
Speech: Lee Kristen
Dance: Steve Kallens (jazz)

SPECIAL SKILLS    Gymnastics, marathon runner, speak fluent French and Italian

### For Actors with Little or No Professional Experience

If you've just gotten out of school or have had little professional experience, it's best not to lie about it. You should include a paragraph or two in your cover letter telling the agent about the work you've done in school (school productions or community theater). It's perfectly alright to share your enthusiasm and determination in the letter, but always keep the tone professional, never desperate.

It might go something like this:

> I've been in New York City for less than a year. Prior to coming here, I studied theater at Emerson College in Boston. I received my bachelor of science degree in Theater Arts. While at Emerson, I played the lead in *Peer Gynt* for our junior year, main-stage production. In my senior year I played Tony in *West Side Story.* I also worked at the Theater Company of Boston as an apprentice.
>
> I am presently studying acting with Uta Hagen at H.B. Studio, singing with Charles Dewinn at the Elonard Conservatory, and dance (jazz technique) at Luigi's. Since arriving here, I've done two showcases. I played Jimmy Porter in *Look Back in Anger* (A.T.A. Theater) and Renauld in *The Crazy Cages*, a new play, at Theater for the New City. I've enclosed some reviews of my work for your consideration.
>
> I feel strongly that if I can get the auditions, I can book the jobs. I'm ready to be sent out. I'd like to meet with you at your earliest convenience to discuss representation. I'll call you at your office at the beginning of the week. I look forward to meeting with you.

# Mailing Campaigns and Promotional Marketing

**C**reating your own mailing campaign can be one of the smartest and most effective ways to promote yourself as an actor. Most casting directors and agents prefer not to be telephoned or visited in person, making it challenging for the actor to maintain contact with them. Mailing provides a nonintrusive and professional means of presenting yourself. It enables you to organize your thoughts and can eliminate a lot of the helpless feelings that occur in this business. It's a way that you can plan and have some control of your presentation. It is a means of developing (and establishing) a good, working relationship with agents and casting directors.

### Getting Your Word Out

Many actors do not have the time, the patience, or the discipline necessary to maintain an ongoing weekly or monthly mailing campaign and hire promotional marketing companies to keep their campaigns going.

According to Michael Neeley, co-owner of Actors' Mailings and Promotional Marketing, a New York–based company, "The majority of actors will try a mailing (large or small) one time: and if they don't get dramatic results, they never do it again. Then they wonder why their career becomes stagnant, why they can't seem to get an agent or a job."

According to Neeley, "most actors, at one time or another, have seen a performance for which they would have been a better casting choice, both in talent and type. What separates the actor that got the role from the actor that was 'right' for the role? There's a good chance that it boiled down to mailings."

A good mailing is sent to all the casting directors and agents that you'd like to meet. It is made up of your picture and résumé and a professional, cordial, and interesting cover letter.

### What a Good Cover Letter Is and What It Can Do for You

Hal Hochhauser, the owner of Shakespeare Mailing Service, says "The headshot shows what you look like and the résumé lists related background and experience. Very important items, but on their own they can create a somewhat impersonal appearance considering the personal nature of our business and the importance of this introduction. It's the cover letter that gives you a voice, personality, and a chance to convey your thoughts."

In the absence of personal contact, the cover letter becomes your smile, your sincerity, and your way to talk to the buyers and sellers of talent. It's an opportunity to share information that may not be on your résumé, or to highlight important achievements that might be missed as they hastily scan the résumés that daily cross their desks. It's a chance to help strangers know your career path, understand your motivations and commitments, gain rapport, and perhaps be motivated to call you for a personal meeting or audition.

The cover letter also answers many unasked questions that agents and casting directors might have, such as, Is this person intelligent, focused, realistic, and understanding of the business? or, Are her thoughts scattered, expectations based on fantasy, and her presentation sloppy and poorly thought out? A good cover letter conveys a lot and can be as important to the success of a mailing as the picture and résumé itself.

People tend to work with people they like, and good communication can facilitate your ability to create good business relationships. A personalized letter becomes a one-to-one communication that can make your reader feel important and your message more meaningful and influential. It tells the reader you recognize his value to your career and it maximizes your chance of getting a response.

### What Should Be Included in a Good Cover Letter

A good cover letter should be direct, professional, cordial, and succinct. The following information should be provided for casting directors and agents:

- State what it is you want and why you're writing this letter.
- Briefly tell them a bit about what you've been doing recently, highlighting important successes (not obviously listed on your résumé).
- Don't tell them the story of your life!
- Briefly let them know your goals, future plans, and expectations. (Naturally, keep this positive and upbeat, with realistic goals.)
- If you have made some good casting director contacts while seeking work, feel free to attach a note with their names. (Tell the truth, they may call them!)
- As you complete the letter, mention that you will call them sometime in the next week to arrange an appointment. (And do that!)
- End your letter with an expression such as, "With warm regards" or "Sincerely."

### An Example of a Good Cover Letter

June 14, 1998

Contact name
Agency name
Address
City, State, Zip

Dear Ms. So-and-so,

I am currently seeking new representation, and would like to meet with you to discuss the possibility of working with you. Although I presently have commercial representation (freelancing with Cunningham, Escott, Dipene and Associates), I would consider signing "across-the-board" if that's your agency's policy.

There are two important issues I would like to mention that are not apparent on my résumé. First of all, I have been making my living as an actor for the last couple of years. In addition, in the short time that I've been in New York City I have been developing contacts. Many of the interviews and auditions I get are through personal sources. Ninety percent of the work that I book is through my own efforts. I don't say this to downplay the need for representation, but rather to express to you my personal motivation and aggressiveness. I firmly believe that, with your representation, I would be able to earn a six-figure income. There are simply too many audition opportunities passing me by.

On that note and for your reference, I have attached a list of the casting directors/offices that are familiar with my work.

I will follow up with a phone call next week to arrange an appointment. If that is inconvenient, or if you would like to meet sooner, please don't hesitate to contact me. I look forward to speaking with you in person.

With warm regards,

The Actor

### The Value of Postcards in Your Ongoing Mailings

Generally, actors will get more work from their postcard mailings than from their headshots. According to Hal Hochhauser at Shakespeare Mailing Service, the reason for this is because "postcards are mailed more frequently. Agents and casting directors often tell you to keep in touch with them by postcards. They (postcards) cost less to mail than eight-by-tens and are less expensive to reproduce; you save on envelopes and postage; they're easier to prepare—no gluing, stapling, stuffing, or sealing; and the most important reason, the way they're handled by agents and casting directors.

"Offices get so much mail that they cannot physically save and file pictures/résumés that aren't used. Compared to postcards, they're cumbersome to manage and take up a lot of room. Postcards are small and can easily be stacked on a shelf or stored in a drawer. Some agents/casting directors keep categorized card files on their desks. When a specific type is sought, they just thumb though the cards, pulling out any that may be appropriate. Compared to your eight-by-ten, your postcard stands a better chance of being saved, thereby increasing your chance of being called at some future date from a picture you send today.

"Regular mailings, with messages that highlight your qualifications and experience, keep your face familiar and phone number handy, increasing the chance of being called when someone of your type is needed."

### What to Say on Your Postcards

- Make sure it's properly addressed with the correct spelling of the casting director's name.
- Keep it legible.
- Keep it very brief (you have about six to eight seconds).
- Make it friendly but businesslike (not too personal).
- Always sign your card.

### Examples of Postcard Notes

1.

Dear Jane,
    I am presently touring nationally with *Cats*. We hit Chicago this week. Hope all is well in NYC.
    I will be back in town in late May.

All my best,
Joan

Jane Doe Casting
115 South Street
Suite 205
New York, NY 10036

**2.**

Dear Ms. Doe,

Just wanted to keep you posted on my latest work. I recently completed my demo reel—which included footage from *Law and Order*, *All My Children*, and *The Cosby Show*.

If you'd like to view it, please give me a call.

All the best,
Bernie

**3.**

Dear Jane,

Join us for a downtown night of up-tempo music. Come hear me sing at Voices at Nell's—located at 246 West Fourteenth Street (between Seventh and Eighth Avenues) on Tuesday, June 11, at 8:00 P.M.

Hope to see you there,
Gwen Sheridan

**4.**

Dear Jane,

I just got back from Chicago where I was doing an industrial for Pacific Bell. I'm back in town, ready to go to work, and hope to hear from you soon.

Sincerely,
Michael Boxton

## The Marketing Aspect of Actor's Mailings

Repetition and frequency are essential elements in all successful advertising. Any marketing professional can tell you, it's a numbers business. You have to increase the public awareness to sell the product. The "public" in this case being casting directors and agents, while the "product" is the actor. Coca-Cola is a household name. Yet, the Coca-Cola company still advertises because it knows that buyers needs change on a daily basis. The product needs to be constantly in their face. What Coca-Cola is saying is, Yes, you have other options—but drink Coke. With their constant reminders, actors are saying, Think of me. Remember me. Use me.

It's been said that casting directors only forget about you if you let them. Two very simple promotional tools are constantly in effect during the actor's mailings: (1) product recognition—casting directors must know "who" you are; and (2) product credibility—through your constant mailings to them, you become more viable.

Casting director Shannon Klassel of Donald Case Casting states, "We cast many jobs, such as MTV promos and other projects calling for new faces, from photos sent directly to our office. Any actor, particularly one new to the business, who doesn't do his or her mailings on a regular basis isn't tending to his or her career."

In the words of the great Milton Berle, "If opportunity doesn't knock, build a door."

### Grass-Roots Publicists

The following promotional marketing companies are experienced in helping actors with their mailing campaigns.

### Shakespeare Mailing Service
### 311 West Forty-third Street, New York, NY 10036
### (212) 956-MAIL

This company has been in business for over eleven years. It has more than five thousand clients and an office staff of about ten. The service does mailings from its contact lists or yours. It sets up various lists according to the actor's specific needs (for example, List A for New York agents, B for regional theaters, and C for L.A.) and has different mailing schedules or messages for each. Industry movement is tracked by computer to help keep your file current. The company also assists actors in creating that all-important cover letter. According to owner Hal Hochhauser: "The headshot and résumé are a perfect represen-tation of who you are and what you've done, but they're static. We help you create a personalized cover letter that bridges the gap, connects you to the specific casting director. You should follow that initial résumé/headshot campaign with postcards on a regular basis. As you know, each casting director receives sometimes hundreds of pieces of mail a day. You only have two to six seconds to catch that agent's or casting director's eye. We help actors with their postcards as well. Our clients book more work more often from postcard mailings (as compared to headshot mailings)."

### Actor's Mailings and Promotional Marketing (AM and PM Inc.)
### 630 Ninth Avenue, Suite 1410, New York, NY 10036
### (212) 307-9420

Michael Neeley, owner of Actors' Mailing and Promotional Marketing, explains: "Our first goal is to modify your way of looking at yourself and the business you strive to succeed in. This includes the acknowl-edgment of the actor as a product. Just as any other product competing in the marketplace, the actor must have a well-developed, long-term marketing plan." The consultants at AM and PM Inc. work with actors on a one-to-one basis to develop their personal marketing program, while teaching them the basics of self-promotion. The company's program includes things like helping actors to develop a polished résumé, a concise cover letter, a tailored mailing list, and a customized mailing strategy. It handles all aspects of the plan including labor, supplies, and postage.

### TVI Actors Studio
### 14429 Ventura Blvd., Suite 118, Sherman Oaks, CA, 91423
### (818) 784-6500
### 165 West Forty-sixth Street, New York, NY 10036
### (212) 302-1900.

Owner Alan Nusbaum was a talent agent for Cunningham, Escott, Dipene and Associates for almost a decade. He noticed how misguided actors were about the business side of the entertainment industry. He set up TVI (Talent Ventures Incorporated) out of that need. TVI puts together résumés and cover letters for members, and provides them with up-to-date industry mailing lists and labels. Actors are drilled on the names of casting directors, and are advised on matters such as headshots and postcards. They can attend casting seminars (chapter 15) and are provided with rehearsal space for practices. All of his teachers also work in the entertainment business as casting directors, producers, directors, and the like. TVI also schedules a yearly talent tour called "Broadway to Hollywood," in which actors go to Los Angeles for one week and audition in front of thirty casting directors.

**Henderson's Mailing Labels**
**360 East Sixty-fifth Street, New York, NY 10021**
**(212) 472-2292; fax (212) 472-5999**
**www.hendersonenterprises.com**

Sue Henderson created this company in 1983 and says it's the "original" actor mailing label list company. Her lists include: Major Mailer—all casting directors in New York, including soaps, series, independent casting directors, ad agencies, and production houses that keep files (there are also smaller versions of this list); New York Soaps; Casting Directors; Production Companies; Model Commercial Print; and Photographers. Henderson also has a Mailing List Setup. This service allows you to create your own list using her database.

# CHAPTER 6

# *Personal Marketing*

In his book *How to Market Yourself,* Michael Dainard defines marketing as "a social and managerial process by which individuals and groups obtain what they need and want through creating and exchanging products and value with others." Dainard says that "marketing has been with us since the beginning of human existence. Whenever you have two or more human beings together, competition sets in and someone starts trying to market something to one of the others. The first recorded example of brilliant marketing, though not necessarily of a good product, took place in the Garden of Eden, when the serpent convinced Eve to try the apple. Eve in turn marketed the apple to Adam."

Dainard points out that "as children we start doing our test marketing very early. We try different forms of persuasion until we find the ones that work best for us. Then we try our early successes on our other family members and friends. Sometimes we find out these strategies don't work on all people at all times, and have to develop new ones for different people and situations.

"This is an early and valuable marketing lesson. We have to use different marketing techniques on different people to get what we want. When we grow older, we use forms of marketing to get a girl/boyfriend or a wife/husband. Are we not using marketing tools when we dress up to impress and win the target of our affections (packaging)? What about the words and speeches we use (audio)? The flowers, candies, movies, and presents (promotion)?"

### Actor "Product" Marketing

Lee K. Bohlen, a professional-life coach, who holds workshops for actors, says it's "very important that actors think of themselves as a 'product.' Once they do, they must then figure out which marketplace they want to sell their product (themselves) to. They must also figure out a way that they can do this most effectively. One of the problems is that many actors think successful marketing is simply developing your craft. They take acting classes, dance classes, singing classes, etc., and feel that if they're well trained and talented, they'll just be 'discovered.' That, quite often, is just a myth. They forget that this is a business, an industry. They leave out the part about being a businessperson."

### Buying and Selling in the Marketplace

When Bohlen refers to "the marketplace," she is referring to the commercial world, the soap world, TV, and stage. "Actors can get further faster in their careers if they specify which market they want to go to. Within our industry there are casting directors and agents that only work in commercials. There are casting directors and agents that just work in stage, TV, and film. If you can specify where you think you can break-in the easiest, you can identify those people that you need to sell to. For instance, if you decide that you're a good commercial type, you step into 'research and development,'" says Bohlen. You watch and study commercials. You make sure that your product identifies with that commercial. The actor's job is to find an effective way to be "identified with that (commercials) market."

### How Nabisco Marketed the Oreo Cookie

To demonstrate the actor's dilemma, Bohlen uses the example of how Nabisco marketed the Oreo cookie. "They took this newly created Oreo cookie to an advertising agency. Within an advertising agency there's three major divisions. First of all, there's research and development. In research and development they study the product (the Oreo cookie) and identify all of the product's weaknesses and flaws. Then they develop the product until it becomes better.

"Next, the Oreo cookie goes to the marketing division. The marketing division takes the cookie just as it is. They go out to the public and tell them all the wonderful things about it, its strengths. It's the marketing division's job to sell the cookie.

"The third division, the production department, keeps producing the cookie.

"An actor has to become all three of those divisions for himself, since the actor is the product he's trying to sell. However, having the ability to stand back and become your own research and development department, your own marketing department, and your own product department is sometimes very difficult for actors."

### The Buy/Sell Line

Bohlen says that "in any business there is a buy/sell line. In show business, agents, managers, and actors are all on the sell side. Casting directors, producers, and writers are all on the buying side of the line. What actors tend to do is keep trying to sell to people on their own side of the buy/sell line. They keep trying to sell to the agents and the managers."

Bohlen strongly advises against that. "Actors should learn to become their own research and development division, their own marketing division, and their own product division. They should sell directly to the producers, the directors, the casting directors, and the writers. Work from the top down."

### Defining Your Type

According to Lee K. Bohlen, "Actors tend to stay in the place where casting directors and agents identify them. They are categorized as young mom, young leading man, business exec, etc. We all have qualities that are beneath these surface labels.

"For example, think about Jack Nicholson. You can describe all the roles that he's played but there's one thing that he brings to everything he does. That one thing is his 'real type.' In Nicholson's case, that real type can be described as 'dangerous and violent.' It's something you see in all of his work. It's not something that he does or has to do. He brings these qualities to everything that he plays."

When an actor can identify his real type (the type that he is even when standing still), then he can really begin his self-marketing campaign. Starting with his mailing campaign, all his future marketing should always reflect who he is. Agents specifically need to know who actors really are, typewise. The clearer the actor is about his type, the easier it will be for the agent to know exactly what to send him out on.

When you're first breaking into the business, you'll move further and faster if you can hone in on your biggest strength. Sally Field realized this early in her career by playing roles like the Flying Nun and Gidget. She sold that one thing (innocent and lovable) completely. Meg Ryan's "charm" is another example. She can stand still and she's charming and you love her.

### Finding Your Type in Television Commercials

Karen Kayser, a commercial casting director at Steve and Linda Horn Casting, feels that "there is a certain way in which you are perceived through the television set. This perception is often different from how you (the actor) perceive yourself." She teaches seminars that bring "actors to the mind-set of the viewer."

Kayser explains: "In trying to be all things to all people, actors make their biggest mistake. They come across as a smiling, one-dimensional, bland being with no personality. In the first second of a commercial, if the viewer is not taken by the commercial, that viewer will move on to another channel.

"There has been a major shift in the advertising business to find actors who have more definition, more personality," says Kayser. In previous years they wanted generic types; not anymore. You must find out who you are in front of the camera. The camera takes a two-dimensional picture of you, re-creating it through the TV monitor, and this is the image that the viewer gets. How you are perceived by people is a major factor in commercials. How do you see me? Actors need an outside source to give them feedback as to how they're being perceived. We are all stuck in our own mind-set about ourselves. Putting yourself on videotape and then looking at the tape is one way to step outside of yourself, but even that is somewhat limited. You still see through I-me. I try to help people discover how they are being perceived visually. Commercials are not about your inner soul. They're about how you are visually perceived and whether you'll be believable as the mailman, or the librarian, etc. Wardrobe, hairstyles, makeup, are all part of the believability factor."

### An Image Consultant

Once you've honed in on your specific type and know which market-place you're interested in pursuing, you may want to seek out an image consultant to assist you in wardrobe, hairstyle, etc. Generally the image consultants' fees vary from $300 to $750.

After several in-depth discussions with a client, the image consultant helps the client to present himself in the most suitable way for his specific type. By going through the client's present wardrobe, the image consultant eliminates clothes that are not the correct style for the specific image that the actor is trying to sell. The image consultant will go clothes shopping with the actor to help him find the most appropriate wardrobe for his new look. She'll help the actor with the best makeup and hairstyles. Don't think image consultants are just for women. Many men have found working with an image consultant to be a rewarding and profitable experience.

Laurie Krauz, a successful image consultant, feels that her role is like that of a teacher. "I give my clients information about their body types and about how to translate that information into merchandise that they find in the marketplace. Essentially, they're trying to marry three things: their body types, things they find in the marketplace, and what they do on a daily basis.

"Actors approach the industry with a belief that the art and the art alone ought to be able to get them cast. Unfortunately, we work in an industry where you can't get to the art before the facade is taken in. Decisions are made about who and what you are as a performer based on what you look like the moment you walk in the door. The first thing I say to an actor at an interview is that he needs to view himself as a can of soup on a shelf in a supermarket. He needs to get his team of advisers together (himself) to answer a few very important questions. What is the soup? What is the flavor of the soup? What kind of packaging will best reflect that flavor? We assume that the flavor is good. That is not what the packaging is about. We have to somehow attract the people walking down the grocery aisle to pick our can of soup off the shelf.

"If you take Katharine Hepburn on one end of the continuum and Marilyn Monroe on the other end, you'll notice that one is very angular and one is very soft and curvy. These are two very different body types, the extremes, you might say. What I try to help actors do is find where they are on this continuum. Really what we're doing is looking at bone structure. The world views us in a certain way because of the way we look. And because the world looks at you a certain way, you develop a certain personality. The Napoleonic complex grew out of the way the man looked—short.

"With actors, type is all physical, it's all body line. The actor playing Dracula is not someone short and delicately boned. Basically, people who are shorter, more curved, or, in the case of men, more triangular torsoed are the softer body types. We generally relate to them as softer, more delicate, more romantic. That's how they're usually cast, in the less aggressive sort of roles. Generally speaking, the more angular people are cast in the more dangerous kind of roles. It's almost like we are all in agreement about what type is, and the psychology of the impact of bone structure.

"It's important for the actors to come up with the best type for themselves—a type that they feel is totally them, so that they can embody it with every inch of their skin.

"I always ask actors to list three roles that they'd be right for in the medium that you've chosen.

"Once we decide on what 'flavor of soup' you are, we can find the specifics. What colors will represent that? What kind of shapes? Do I wear pants or do I wear a skirt? If I'm a man, do I wear a suit or is that too fancy for me?

"Actors must always maintain a degree of professionalism in how they look. Hair combed, shoes not scuffed, etc. It's all part of the package, their presentation of who they are."

# Getting and Preparing for Interviews and Auditions

**T**wo things that almost every actor must constantly do in the entertainment industry is to go to interviews (sometimes called "taking meetings" in Los Angeles) and auditions. Many actors find interviews and auditions everything from challenging to almost unbearable. There are those few fortunate actors who love interviews and find auditioning to be "just another wonderful opportunity to perform." Good for them, they're the lucky few.

### What Is an Interview?

An interview is a meeting with a casting director, director, producer, or agent. It's an opportunity for that person to get to know you. It's very rare that an actor is cast just from an interview, but it does happen (more in England than here). Some casting directors schedule general interviews on a regular basis.

### How to Get an Interview

Usually the best way to get an interview is through personal recommendation. As you've heard, I'm sure, in show business it's "who you know" quite often that can get you in the door.

The second way to get an interview is to contact casting offices or agents by mail. Send your picture and resume with a good cover letter specifically requesting an interview. Unfortunately, more often than not, you won't hear back from them. But occasionally you do (especially if you're gorgeous or very interesting looking, or wrote a letter that intrigued them).

The third way to get an interview is to call them on the phone and request one. But before lifting that receiver:

- Make sure you're in a good mood and feeling positive.
- Be prepared to be businesslike, direct, and brief.
- Take a breath, dial . . . and go for it!
- Understand that if you don't get past the receptionist, it's nothing personal, and it shouldn't be taken as a rejection.

### You Get the Interview: What Are You So Afraid Of?

That casting director has agreed to meet with you for an interview. Hurrah! Many actors, however, become filled with fear and trepidation as the day of the interview draws near. Why? They worry because they don't know what will happen at the interview and fear the worst. Questions like, What will she be like? Will she like me? What should I talk about? What shouldn't I say? What should I wear? Should I dress upscale or be more casual? The uncertainty can terrorize you. The best way to combat this fear is to find out everything you can about the person you're going to meet and the office that you're going to. The solution to your fear is simple—prepare.

### Preparing for the General Interview: First the Facts

Find out as much as you can about the person you're going to meet. If it's an agent, try to find out who some of the agency's clients are, how long the agency has been in the business, what type of reputation it has, if it accepts videotapes, if it has offices on both coasts, what it's franchised in (theater, TV, film, commercials)—everything. Ask around, network, and ask your friends.

If it's a casting director, find out what she's cast in the past, what she's presently casting, and what she's slated to cast in the future. Find out how long the office has been in existence. Does it have offices on both coasts? What type of reputation does it have? Again, research, network, and call your friends. The more you can find out about the person who will be interviewing you, the more comfortable you'll feel. That knowledge will be helpful in alleviating your fears.

### Improvising the Interview

Once you have all the information you can find, the next step is to imagine the situation. When you think about it, most interviews, no matter what they're about, have a certain commonality. They begin when you enter the door; you say hello, you sit down, you talk, you say good-bye, and then you leave. In addition, in some interviews, you're asked to perform a prepared monologue or read some cold copy or sing a prepared song. That's about all that's going to happen. There shouldn't be too many other surprises.

While at home, improvise what you'll say. I use the word "improvise" because the last thing you want is to sound like some kind of machine spewing out memorized facts and information about yourself. Don't rehearse a memorized script, improvise. Remain loose.

You can be assured that interviewers will ask certain basic questions such as, So what have you been up to? and, Tell me about yourself. After looking at your résumé for a moment, they may start chatting with you about a theater that you've mentioned or a director they're familiar with. This is not a quiz! Don't get uptight. Prepare in advance by being very familiar with everything on your résumé. While improvising at home, create imaginary conversations about items on your résumé. Try to be positive in everything that you say. Even in the case of those horrible professional experiences that you may have had, give them a positive spin. Nobody wants to hear an actor whining or complaining at an interview.

One of the great residuals of doing all this preparation before the interview is the feeling of confidence you'll have when you actually go in for the interview. You know that you've prepared to the best of your ability. And even though you still may be a little nervous, you'll be a lot more confident.

### Types of Interviews and How to Prepare for Them

There are several types of interviews for which you may be called in. I'll briefly explain what some of them are and how you can best prepare for them.

First there's a commercial interview. Sometimes, rather than having an audition for a TV commercial, casting directors will have a commercial interview instead. The best way to prepare for this is to find out as much information as you can about the product and the specific commercial you're up for. Ask your agent to fill you in on what he knows. If you feel that what he knows isn't sufficient, then politely, professionally call the production office. Ask questions such as, Will this be a comedic commercial? and, Will it be scripted? Find out as much as you can. Whatever you learn will be helpful. Unfortunately, many times the agent won't be able to tell you too much. The best you can do is try.

Next there's the theatrical interview. This is when you're auditioning for a play to be performed in a theater. The more you know about the particular play (not just your role or the scenes you're in), the better. Again, ask your agent specific questions about the play and the character for which you'll be auditioning. If the play is published, get a copy. If it isn't, call the casting office, and politely ask if you could come by and get a copy to read in advance. If not, could you at least come in earlier the day of your interview to read it? Find out as much as you can about the director and producer for whom you'll be auditioning. What other plays have they done? What are their backgrounds? Knowing as much as you can about them can be fodder for a good conversation when you meet with them at the interview.

Once you have some information about the play and the character, it's always wise to dress accordingly. In some situations (period dramas, historical plays), actors have made the mistake of costuming themselves. That is, rather than dressing in a manner that suggests the appropriate wardrobe, they'll rent the actual costume for that period. Aside from perhaps looking somewhat foolish, you may come across as being too desperate. I wouldn't advise that. *Suggesting* the wardrobe is all you need to do.

In the case of soap opera or episodic TV interviews, find out as much as you can about the show. If you're familiar with the show, don't hesitate to tell the interviewer how much you've enjoyed watching the show (and specifically tell them why).

For a movie interview, see if you can read the script in advance (more likely than not you won't be able to). Once again, make sure that you get as much information from your agent as possible about the movie (and specifically your character).

### What Is an Audition?

As one actor I spoke with recently joked, "Auditions are the bane of my existence. If it wasn't for them, I'd be a star." For some actors, auditioning is an unpleasant, frightening experience.

Simply put, auditions are an opportunity for you to "show them what you got." You may be asked to perform material that you've prepared, such as a monologue or a scene, or you may read from a script for a director, producer, casting director, or agent.

In the case of reading from the script, you'll either be given the material in advance or right before the audition (a cold reading).

### How to Get an Audition

Aside from getting an audition through an agent, the same ways mentioned for interviews apply—that is, through personal connections, by writing, or by phoning. You may also find out about them on the bulletin boards at Actors Equity, SAG (Screen Actors Guild), or AFTRA (American Federation of Television and Radio Artists). Sometimes a friend will give you a tip about a specific audition that you can follow up on. And then there's always the trade papers such as *Backstage* and *Variety* that list auditions.

### Preparing for the Audition

Many of the solutions to your fears for auditions are similar to the ones I discussed in the section on interviews. Once again, the more you know about the play, the style of the play, the playwright, the character, the people who are auditioning you (the casting director, the director, the producer), and even the room in which you'll be auditioning, the better.

If it's to be a cold reading, practice your cold-reading skills at home. If the audition is to take place on a large theater stage, be prepared to project your voice and energy. If it's for a movie or TV, be prepared to be more intimate; make your movements more subtle.

If you've been asked to bring in a prepared monologue, make sure you know it inside out. Learning a new monologue right before an important audition will only add to your tension. You should have a variety of monologues prepared well in advance for all types of auditions. When you start to feel that the monologues you've been doing are stale, make sure you replace them immediately with new ones.

Preparing yourself emotionally for auditions (especially the bigger, more important ones) is a bit trickier. Certainly, you should practice relaxation and positive-thinking techniques prior to all auditions. Remember, having "nerves" isn't a bad thing if the energy is channeled directly into the audition. Each actor must find his own way of coping with the stress and pressure of auditioning. Keep in mind that the auditors really do want you to be good. The better your work, the easier their job will be. They are not the enemy. Many actors approach auditions with the mind-set that they already have the job and now they're just performing it. Confidence is the key. Any way you can create it in yourself for the audition is the best way.

# Videotapes

**M**ore and more casting directors and agents are now accepting videotapes from actors to see their work. One of the first questions many Los Angeles talent agents ask of prospective actor clients is, Do you have a reel? It's become almost as important (particularly in Los Angeles) as having a picture and résumé. Unlike the picture and résumé, however, which can be sent to practically anyone, actors should not send out their "reels" unsolicited.

This six- to seven-minute sampling of an actor's work can give a casting director or agent an initial idea of who the actor is, how he or she looks on screen, and suggest type and range. Certainly it's not fair to say that all the actor's skills will be evident. Videotapes are made up of clips from jobs that the actor previously booked. In most cases, the emphasis was not on showcasing the actor's talent as much as moving the teleplay along, or, in many cases, showcasing the show's star. Hopefully, the actor will be able to find a few moments from these taped jobs that will show at least some degree of his or her talent. Actors ask, What if I have no clips—if I've not yet done any professional work? Should I make up a demo tape of monologues and staged scenes? The answer to that question depends on who you ask. Some agents and casting directors feel that it's a waste of time to make up these "homegrown reels." Others feel that it does have some value, but only if it's very well done (which could be quite expensive) and very carefully thought out.

### Creating Your Reel

In creating your reel, select the best sample clips from any speaking roles you've had on soap operas, films, episodic work, and any on-camera commercial work. If you don't have a copy of a particular show in which you appeared, you should contact the show's production office as soon as possible to see if it can provide you with a copy of your scene. You can get copies of TV commercials you've worked on from the ad agency (once it's been aired).

When editing material for your reel, you should find a professional, well-recommended videotape-editing company. Amateur work usually looks like amateur work. It's not worth shortchanging your career just to save a few dollars. Go for the pro.

After selecting the best six to seven minutes of your material, the editing studio will transfer it to a three-quarter-inch professional quality tape. From that tape, they'll make your three-quarter-inch "master," and from that master, you'll be making all the half-inch video cassettes to be handed out to casting directors and agents.

Videotape editing can be very expensive. Generally, it will run from $250 to $500. The better prepared you are before you walk into the studio, the more you'll save in the end.

All of your artistic decisions regarding the tape should be made well in advance. One way to prepare is to use a stopwatch to determine exactly how much time each segment runs and figure out where you'd like it placed on the reel. Be open, however, to any suggestions that the video editor makes.

### What Should Go on Your Reel?

- Start with your name and any contact information. Some actors follow that section with a headshot.
- Select scenes that feature your character. Many times you're hired to perform in scenes where your character is supportive of the lead (and therefore receives little camera time). Which-

ever scene you choose, make sure that there are at least a few
good shots of you.

- Select scenes that show you in a relationship. Quite often, how
  well you act is judged by how honestly you *react*.
- Try to show range of character and variety of type on your reel.
  The more versatile you can show them you are, the more
  future work possibilities there will be.
- Always keep your reel updated. You should be revising it
  periodically, especially if you get a great scene that showcases
  your talent.
- Many actors end their reels by repeating the opening credits—
  name, headshot, and contact information.
- Something else to keep in mind: the people viewing your reel
  see hundreds of them. If possible, try to entertain them.

### A Reel for the Neophyte

Suppose you haven't done any professional work yet. As I mentioned
earlier, the industry is divided as to whether a homegrown reel is of
any value. If you do decide to make one and plan on submitting it to
specific casting directors or agents, I advise that you let them know
beforehand that it's made up of staged work. Give them the option as
to whether or not they'd like to see it. Don't surprise them.

When shooting your own material, consider the following:

- It's always better to select material from something that you've
  previously worked on. This is not the time to try out new
  material. Choose something from a production you once
  worked on, something you've developed in acting class or with
  your coach, or even some original material (if you honestly
  feel it's good enough).
- Try to keep your selections contemporary. Classical styles tend
  to look a bit stagey on camera, and unless performed with
  tremendous flair, can make you look like a ham.
- Try to choose material that is physically contained, shows
  some range, and shows you at your best. Select roles that are
  within your age range and that you could conceivably be cast
  in. This is not a time to "stretch."
- All aspects of the production (lighting, sound, makeup, wardrobe, etc.) should be worked out (prior to the day of the shoot).

### Should I Include Taped Segments from Live Professional Performances That I Did?

Again the answer is, it depends. Generally, these tapings emphasize the play or production, not the actor. Also, you don't usually get the close-ups that you can get in film and TV. Your voice quality may not be too good. And, finally, the quality of these videotapes is usually a bit more grainy. When transferred to a reel, they lose even more clarity, sometimes making the picture seem slightly blurry or muddy. It's up to you. Remember, you can always change your mind in the studio if you discover that it's not the quality that you want on your reel.

### Who to Send Your Reel To

Alright, you finally have the reel that you feel represents your talent. But then you ask, Who do I send it to? As I mentioned earlier, unlike a picture and résumé (that can be sent to practically anyone in the industry), you must target where you send your reel. First of all, only send it to those people who have expressed interest in seeing it. Next, buy a copy of the *Ross Report* (and other casting books). Agents and casting directors are usually very clear as to whether they accept unsolicited videotapes. If it says "Don't send unsolicited videotapes"—don't!

### Tips for Keeping Track of Your Tapes

Here are some things to keep in mind when sending out your video-tapes.

- Make sure they always have your name and your address on them. That means on the tapes as well as the boxes they're in. Many actors also glue a picture postcard to their videotapes.
- Keep a log of where all material has been sent. Include the names, addresses, and dates of material sent and when it was returned to you. Material will only be returned if you include a self-addressed, stamped envelope.
- After a few weeks, if you haven't heard from the agents or casting directors, give them a call and politely inquire as to whether they've had a chance to see your material yet.

# Interviews with Videographers and Video Editors

In this chapter, I've interviewed several videographers and video editors. Videographers shoot your performances live (scenes and monologues in their studios). Video editors edit preexisting material (work from jobs you've done previously). Once again, I strongly suggest that you only have your reel done professionally.

BEN BRYANT (**BB**) is a freelancer video editor. Most of the work he's done is editing preexisting footage (commercials, movies, segments from TV shows, soap operas). He's been a freelance producer for about twenty years. Bryant has produced about eight hundred to nine hundred commercials in the last fifteen years. He's done everything from McDonald's to Miller beer. He has been doing freelance editing for actors for about five years. What he prefers doing is original taping (for actors who haven't done any professional on-camera work).

JOHNATHAN PERRY (**JP**) at Video Portfolio Productions has done most of his work over the years editing actors' video reels, helping them select and organize material, and giving their reels a professional and high-quality look. Video Portfolio Productions has been in business for fifteen years.

JOANNA (JE) at Jan's Video Editing. Jan Natarno began this company in the late 1970s. He was one of the first people to tape shows off the air so that actors could get copies. He started a library of taped soaps and prime-time shows that today is quite extensive. Jan's is one of the oldest places in Hollywood for video editing. Joanna now runs Jan's and works closely with actors in selecting and organizing material for their reels.

---

**What general suggestions and advice do you have for actors before making their videotapes?**

**BB:** First of all, for any studio work, hire a professional videographer to record your work. Before booking anyone, always look at a demo reel. Amateur videos generally look like amateur videos. The problem with shooting it yourself with a home video camera is technical (incorrectly framing a shot, footage severely over- or underexposed, focus jumping all over the place).

When selecting segments from work you've previously done, make sure that *you* are the emphasis of the segment, not the other actors. This is your showcase, no one else's. If you can get the production copy, don't tape it yourself from TV. The quality is generally inferior. Don't do too much fancy stuff, just brief intros to each segment.

As far as us shooting work in the studio, it should be very short (monologues about a minute to a minute-and-a-half long). You want to be as prepared as possible. If you're doing a scene, make sure the other actor is as prepped as you are. A scene shouldn't be more than a couple of minutes. Keep the background simple and nonspecific (a black backdrop or seamless photographic paper). Be sure you're well lit. The only thing we should be focused on is you and your performance.

Remember, the purpose of the demo tape is to show as much range as you can in as short a time as possible. Casting directors can tell within fifteen or twenty seconds whether or not you have what they're looking for. You can decide what they watch or they can decide what they watch.

Also, make sure when hiring a videographer to shoot your live performance in a play that they are adept with lighting or sound;

neither of these things can be fixed in an editing studio. When shooting live performances, generally the videographer is shooting from the back of the house. The camera with a built-in mike can hardly pick up the actor's voice. The result will be a poor-quality sound level. Also, you'll get a lot of room tone and you may even hear the camera motor hum. The videographer should use a wireless radio mike or an omnidirectional mike for scenes with several actors in them.

**JP:** You should put a lot of thought into what goes on your reel and in which order. If you don't have too much good work, then maybe it would be better to wait until you do. I've seen too many actors put together a sloppy reel of work that doesn't really feature them. It's a waste of time and money. Also, shorter is better unless you've got a drop-dead dramatic scene.

If you want us to shoot your work while you're performing in a show in the theater, we have to work closely with the lighting designer to get the best quality. We can do a lot with lenses, but you must be well lit.

As to taping performed work in a studio, it generally looks cheesy. Unless you're willing to spend a lot of money, it generally doesn't look that good.

**JE:** The strongest work should come up first because you don't know how long someone will actually view the demo. Keep it as short as possible (five minutes or less). It's worth spending the extra money to get "air checks" (taped on three-quarter-inch tape by a service like Jan's Video Editing). You'll get a much better quality. Casting directors are really just looking to see how well you act. Don't spend unnecessary money on special effects to jazz up your tape.

**What are the biggest mistakes actors make when they bring in their videos to be edited?**

**BB:** The classic is really trying to put too much on the reel. Also, bringing in taped scenes that don't really show them off. Another big mistake that actors make is that they want to add too many special effects to their reels. They want all this stuff at the beginning of the reel, lengthy lead-ins and fancy intros—all unnecessary. As one agent once said to me, "What are they trying to hide?" My feeling about videos is that you have the actor's name at the beginning and *bang* you get right to the material. I also feel you should have the actor's contact number at the end of the reel, not at the beginning. If the actor has the opening title, whether it's *Guiding Light* or *The Terminator*, I'll put that up and *boom*, get right to them in their scene.

**JP:** Many actors come in here and want to preserve the sense of the film (the narrative) on their reels. It can't be done, there's not enough time on your reel. You're not showcasing the film. Remember, the reel should only be five to seven minutes. Think only of your work. Get a three-quarter-tape from the production company (rather than a VHS) for a better quality.

Actors waste a lot of time in the editing studio. They should do all their decision making at home before they get to the studio, otherwise it's going to cost them.

When you shoot your monologues and scenes in a studio, here are some things to remember:

- Don't try to do things that are too elaborate.
- Don't get too caught up in props.
- Don't act as you would on the stage. Video acting, like film acting, should be honest but much smaller than on stage. Usually I'll want to get in close with the camera. If you're too big, it won't look real.
- Don't worry too much about action. Don't do too much physical stuff.
- Don't wear bright red, it bleeds.
- An actor who has dark skin should not wear bright white shirts. All the light goes to the shirt, which makes it very hard to get your face to expose properly.
- Striped or checked patterns don't come out well on video (they shimmer).

**JE:** Many actors don't have their tapes keyed up to their scenes. We waste valuable studio time looking for their scenes. Also, many actors have no idea what they want their tapes to look like. If they have agents, they should confer with them. The agent will be shopping it.

**What should and shouldn't an actor expect from a professional videographer? What should/shouldn't an actor expect from a video editor?**

**BB:** The first questions I'm usually asked are, How much will this cost? and, How long will it take? It's impossible to answer these questions because it really depends on the material the actor has selected and how well prepared he is. I can tell you how long it *should* take to shoot a one-minute monologue. But I can't know if you fluff your lines, if you'll want it shot from nine different angles, etc. The same is true for editing someone's reel.

Some things you should look for and ask yourself when looking at the videographer's reel of studio work:

- How does the actor look on camera?
- What do you think of the studio's lighting? Is the lighting appropriate for the scene? Is the lighting for the serious material the same as the lighting for the comedic material?
- Is the background setting distracting? You don't want to see bad shadows or inappropriate things (like the edge of somebody's desk, or a bookcase).

One thing an actor shouldn't expect is for the video editor to fix a bad performance. Many of the things we discussed (bad lighting, bad sound, etc.) can't be fixed. Also, please remember when you videotape a show from TV on your VCR, *always* record at standard speed and on a high-quality tape. The editor can't fix the tape once it's been recorded at too slow a speed. It's always good to try to get a copy right from the master. You'll get a better-quality reel. Contact the producers and see if they can get you a copy.

**JP:** Digital (computer-based) editing is becoming more and more the thing these days; we can do a lot more. But even with that, you shouldn't think that we can help you if your tape is of a poor quality. One thing I can do sometimes is edit a scene to favor your work. Actors should also expect a studio to have basic titling capabilities.

**JE:** Don't expect editors to read your mind. You must know what you want and be clear about it. Editors usually have a really good eye and can be of immense help if allowed. The scenes done in the studio usually look like a home video. We don't really recommend them. If you must do them, keep them simple and be well rehearsed.

### Generally what are your fees?

**BB:** Most video editors charge an hourly rate. My hourly rate is $60. The average length it takes to make up a five- to six-minute reel is just over three hours.

**JP:** We charge $65 an hour for editing. If you want to do it online, we charge $95. If you want us to shoot your work here in the studio, we charge $95.

**JE:** We charge about $60 an hour for editing.

# *Voice-overs*

**W**hat exactly is a voice-over? The term "voice-over" originally came into use when actors had to put their "voice over a motion picture." According to David Zema, voice-over specialist, it is "Any voice heard over visuals where you do not see the person talking. For example, the voice or announcer you hear introduce a television network news program or the voice you hear on a television commercial telling you about a sale at the local department store are both voice-overs. Narrations of films or multimedia presentations can also be considered voice-overs. Today, radio commercials are also called voice-overs. Additionally, voice-over performers must have the ability to read copy in a natural way so as to make it sound as if it is being spoken spontaneously in a believable, sincere, and trusting manner by someone who is highly involved personally and understands the message and can communicate it to a specific listener for a specific reason or reasons. Effective voice-overs for commercials, recorded novels, and radio drama require the ability to create moods and express the appropriate emotions needed to convey the author's message."

### Are Voice-overs for You?

Actors who have been told that they have interesting or unusual voices, or that their voice has an unusual pitch or accent, should look into this very lucrative field. The job of the voice-over actor is quite simply to sell a product. Because your face is never seen, this work has a built-in anonymity to it, perfect for those actors who are uncomfortable in front of the camera. Not everyone, however, is right for voice-over work. So, before rushing out and making up a voice-over demo, I suggest that you check with agents and casting directors you know to see if they feel that you have potential in this field. Also check out some of the voice-over schools and coaches, and ask their opinions. This is a very competitive field. If you honestly feel your voice is special and/or that you're willing to work very hard to develop the necessary skills to be successful, then I say, *Go for it!*

### Nine Tips for Voice-over Success *by David Zema*

- On a daily basis you should listen to professional voices and listen for their performance styles and qualities. Record these voices and try to emulate each performance style.
- Read aloud daily. Books, magazines, newspapers, and even ketchup bottles can be helpful.
- Work on a good tape recorder with a separate microphone.
- Find your own strengths, the copy styles and products your voice is most suited for.
- Project your entire personality into your voice.
- Work on your resonance and diction daily.
- After developing your strengths, work on opening your vocal and performance style range so that you will be more versatile.
- Work with a supportive, positive coach on a regular basis.
- Wait until you have mastered your skills and feel confident about what you have to do before making up a demo. Do not send a homemade demo to the top talent agencies.

### Your Voice-over Demo

The voice-over demo shouldn't be more than a couple of minutes long. It's imperative that you have your best work up front. If the agents don't hear what they want immediately, there is a tendency to turn it off. In your natural voice, do at least a few spots. Variety is the key here. Your voice must be very expressive. You must be able to show emotional, dramatic, and comedic changes. If you can do character work, make sure that each character is as brief as possible. That is, establish the character and then get on to the next one. Whatever type of copy you use (original or professional), make sure that it's appropriate for your type of voice.

You should always have your demo done in a professional studio. It can be a bit pricey, about $700 for the whole thing (including session time in a recording studio), but there are always good deals to be found. Just make sure the level of work is professional.

One thing you need to realize is that your first demo tape is not your *only* demo tape. It's something that's going to change. If the demo tape is working for you, you really don't have to make another one. As you start booking jobs, you'll be using sample clips from your work. Select very wisely when you do this. Make sure the sample features you and shows you off well. You shouldn't put different types of work on one reel. It's basically a field of specialization. In the beginning, try not to be all things to all people. Find what you're best at and put it on the demo. Next, find out who needs what you're best at and then send it to them. (There is much more information on demo tapes in the interviews in the next chapter.)

### How to Get Voice-over Work

Use the various trade sources like the *Ross Report*, David Zema's *Voiceover Marketing Guide and Production Screen Magazine* (Chicago), and *The Standard Directory of Advertising Agencies*. Each area has its own book of listings. There's a national directory called *The Motion Picture, TV, and Theater Directory* (Tarrytown, New York). It comes out twice a year and costs about $8.

Before sending out your demo, it's sometimes best to call first, find out who the casting director is, and ask if you may send it. Naturally, agents are very important contacts; and don't forget producers, ad agencies, and recording studios. Think of your tapes as ads. Once you've mailed them out, you probably won't get them back, although some of the big agencies will return them. You should follow up and call the places you've sent your tapes to. You may realize that one sending of a demo tape and one phone call may not be enough. You have to follow up with a postcard or a note, then a second phone call and a third phone call. If you're an actor who works on camera, you might want to also have your photo on your demo box. Also, you can make rounds (go in person to agents, casting directors, and studios) to drop off your demo. Studios, by the way, are also in a position to recommend you for work. Many producers work out of their homes and might be offended if you show up there, so I don't recommend that you do that.

### Dispelling Voice-over Myths and Misconceptions

So many actors are afraid to look into the lucrative field of voice-overs because of fears of inadequacy or misinformation. Voice-over specialist David Zema says, "I'd like to squelch some of those fears," and provides the following answers to common questions.

- *There is a belief that only strong voices are needed for voice-overs. Is that true?* There is a great demand in voice-overs for comedic and character work. They are always looking for "quirky" and "interesting" voices. There's no doubt, however, that having a good, strong voice is a plus.

- *Another belief is that no one trains for this type of work. Either you're born with a great voice or you're not.* Some people who have been told that they have good or interesting voices have the misconception that all they need to do is open their mouths and sound pretty. Even mellifluous or quirky voices need training. It's not so much the voice, or what you're saying, it's how you say it. Voice-overs are like singing: you have to know how to use your voice.

- *Are voice-overs basically just "reading copy"?* The key is to make it sound natural. It's not always easy to be conversational and enthusiastic under pressure. It takes supreme confidence.

- *You rarely hear women announcers. Is the voice-over field sexist?* There are a lot of women in the voice-over field, especially in cartoons. Women's voices are well suited to cartoons because of their flexibility. I'm not saying that there has never been sexism in the field of voice-overs, but women have made great strides in the past twenty years. Female voices are used more and more.

- *Is training really necessary for voice-over work?* Not knowing how to use your voice correctly can be damaging in the long run. Placing your voice in the throat to deepen the voice is the sign of an amateur and can irritate the throat. It's better to train and develop a natural range and resonance that produces a pleasing voice without tension.

# Interviews with Voice-over Specialists

**D**AVID ZEMA (**DZ**) is a voice-over performer, producer, and coach with fifteen years of experience. His voice can be heard in many commercials, cartoons, and industrials. He has a B.A. in media, and a New York State teacher's license in Broadcast Announcing. He is also a casting consultant and producer.

GLENN HOLTZER (**GH**) teaches voice-overs at Weist-Barron (a theater, television, film school with branches in New York City and Los Angeles) and also does private coaching. He trained as an actor for twenty years and has been teaching for twelve (ten years at Weist-Barron).

---

**What kind of training should an actor have before making a voice-over tape?**

**DZ:** A good voice-over coach can help you where the studio engineer can't. A coach should have a good idea where you are specifically marketable. I personally think the best way for someone to learn voice-overs is private training. A voice-over class can tell you what the basics are, how to handle the copy, how to handle the auditions, how to take direction, teaches warm-up exercises, and teaches the actor the different styles of copy. Private coaching, however, is far more advantageous. You get a lot of microphone time, learn how to take direction, learn different ways to handle the same material, and learn different techniques. A coach can also help you learn where your blocks are and teach you how to sound more natural.

**GH:** Before starting any voice-over training, I think it's important to have an acting background. I think acting classes are very important for the voice-over artist. True, there are some actors who are natural voice-over people and they learn as they go along, but that's very rare. Actors with theater training seem to learn voice-over work faster.

I teach actors to apply their acting work to the script. Don't be fake. You must talk to one person, put your personality into the work, connect to the copy, know the text (you can't just read), and know who you're talking to. The story must have a beginning, middle, and end. Part of what I teach is that you must make it personable, as personal and as conversational as possible through whatever format they're asking for. Whether it's "up energy" or "sexy" or "first person" or "character," your job is to make it believable. The main thing is it must come from you. It's not just announcing and reading well. That's why 95 percent of voice-over performers are actors.

### What is the price range of coaches and classes?

**DZ:** Classes can start as low as $250 for six classes and can go up to $900 or $1,000 for the ones that include a demo tape. Coaches are as low as $40 or $50 and can go as high as $60 or $95 for the top people.

**GH:** Anywhere from $50 to $125 an hour for coaches. Weist-Barron charges $350 for ten classes. Generally, that seems to be about the going rate.

### What things should an actor know before making a demo tape?

**DZ:** Get good, clear guidance. Find someone you trust who can help you. You'll need someone who knows about the market and can help the actor see where he fits in. Sometimes you can't really see that yourself. If you know a casting director or talent agent who knows your work he or she might be of some value to you. Basically, I think that actors make a lot of mistakes with their demo tapes. They rush out and get a voice-over demo without really designing it. Just as people should put in time with their headshots, they should also be selective about their demo tapes. This is a marketing tool, an advertisement for yourself. Actors often go to the first studio they find and do a demo tape without ever asking if the studio does actor voice-over demo tapes. It could be a music studio they've gone to. It wouldn't be appropriate. The studio wouldn't know how to mix the music appropriately, or even know the correct copy. Avoid studios that use a copy file. These pieces of copy have been around forever. That same copy is on many demos.

**GH:** Almost every agent that has come to Weist-Barron to talk to my voice-over class has said that 95 percent of all voice-over tapes that they receive end up in the garbage can. What they're saying is that most voice-over tapes are not good. If the tape is good, you better be able to back it up with a good audition. You must be able to nail a read in the first take (because you only get two or three shots).

**What are the initial expenses in making a demo tape and how much time do you need to allow to set it up?**

**DZ:** Everyone does it differently. There are these places where you can take a six-week class and come out with a demo tape costing you about $1,000. But I definitely say do not do that unless you've already done the private coaching and the other stuff we've talked about. Some studios have package deals. Generally, it can range from about $300 to about $500. It usually takes about two to three hours in the studio. Some places produce the whole thing right there and give it to you then. Other places may make you come back on another day. Generally, the copies can be as low as $1 a tape up to $3 a tape.

**GH:** Actors must be very well prepared before they go into the studio. Make sure that those reads are prepared and down and ready to go. Demos can be made for as little as $250 or $300 and can go as high as

$1,000. For over twelve years I've been doing voice-over demos over at Full House Productions. They do all the demos for Bloom, Cunningham, ICM, Paradigm, all the big agencies. I charge my fee ($65 an hour) and their charge for talent is $75 an hour. It usually takes about three or four hours.

### What would you say the criteria should be for selecting a studio?

**DZ:** It should be a studio that does voice-overs; records voice-overs for radio and TV. Don't go to a music studio or to someone that only does industrials. The engineer should be familiar with voice-overs. He should have recorded auditions as well (so he knows what the casting directors are looking for). He should be comfortable mixing voice-overs, mixing music, sound effects, whatever. You also need someone at the studio who can direct you to know what is currently marketable.

**GH:** It should be a full-service studio, not just a studio that does demo tapes. Use a studio that specifically has had experience doing voice-over demos. Also find a studio that is used to doing ad agency work. Aside from Full House Productions, the only other studio in New York that I recommend is Star Tracks.

### What are agents looking for on a demo tape?

**DZ:** The number one thing is, Is it marketable? "Marketable" in advertising means, What is the current trend? Advertising has trends. Like the Generation X sound is very big now. Some others in the past have been announcers, spokespersons, those kinds of things. In the eighties, a big one was the Molson Golden couple—the flirtatious husband-wife, boyfriend-girlfriend, kind of Stiller and Meara thing. Another one is the guy who was doing the Alamo voice-overs. He had kind of a poetic style that was popular for a while.

**GH:** Anything and everything. Whatever the agent needs for his roster. Whatever style he feels is selling. It really depends on the actor as to what he puts on his demo. If the actor is good with character voices,

I suggest that he highlight that on tape. Range is not necessarily important, conciseness is.

## What do voice-over casting directors look for?

**DZ:** Much of their concern is whether you can handle the job, are at a certain professional level. They certainly can tell from a demo tape whether you're ready.

**GH:** Pretty much what I said before for agents. Also, casting directors usually refer to agents.

## How long should the demo tape be?

**DZ:** A commercial demo is around two minutes long. A promo is really short, under two minutes. A character demo will be a little longer because you have several characters. An industrial tape will be a little longer, closer to three minutes. They want to make sure that you can sustain the reading. Also, the medical tape will be closer to three minutes.

**GH:** A minute-and-a-half to two minutes.

## How many different types of promos are there?

**DZ:** Medical-technical, industrial (financial, training tapes, info-mercials), CD-ROMs, films (under narration), commercial demo, commercial character, and there is cartoon character demos (mostly used in L.A.). Also, if you do foreign languages, have a tape for that. The new tape these days is the promo tape (announcers—big on the cable channels, as well as on talk shows).

**GH:** Now there are commercial demos, promo demos, character demos, and narration demos.

**What kind of money can you make in this field?**

**DZ:** The top people, these promo announcers, make six figures. But there are no residuals, they have to work every day. But, generally, a good voice-over person can make $50,000 to $60,000, up to $100,000 and more.

**GH:** Side money (part time) in voice-overs can go from $10,000 to $15,000 a year (and more). Full time, you can make up to a few million a year—the sky's the limit. There only are a few overnight successes. It usually takes a few years to start making real money. There's probably five hundred or six hundred people in New York trying to get voice-over work today. So, sometimes it can take a while to make some real money in the field.

# Actor Directories

**A**ctor directories are books (and now also on CD-ROM) listing actors' names, photos, contact information, and sometimes a brief mention of some of their more recent credits. The books are categorized by types such as leading man and woman, ingenue, younger leading man, character/comedienne female, character/comedian male, child female, and child male.

Casting directors refer to these books quite often when casting different projects. Every actor should make it a point to be listed in them each year.

The two major casting directories are the following:

### The Academy Players Directory

This directory, known as the industry's casting bible, has been in existence since 1937. About 16,000 actors are listed each year. It's used more often on the West Coast but also lists actors living on the East Coast. The directory lists your name, physical characteristics, representation, specific casting categories, union affiliations, special skills, and professional credits. *The Academy Players Directory* requests that you submit the following:

- A completed submission form. To receive a form you can request one from: *The Academy Players Directory*, 8949 Wilshire Blvd., Beverly Hills, CA 90211-1972; (310) 247-3058.
- An eight-by-ten headshot.
- A check or money order for $25 for each category you want to be listed in. There are three issues per year ($75).

### The Link (The Academy Players Directory Online)

In July 1996, the Academy and Breakdown Services, Ltd., which supplies the entertainment industry with daily information about available acting roles, forged an alliance to develop new ways for agents and casting directors to do their jobs, utilizing rapidly changing technological tools. The resulting new electronic system, The Link, streamlines the photo submission process between talent agents and casting directors. Under the new system, Breakdown Services electronically transmits its daily breakdowns of available acting roles to its clients. Using the photos and résumés from *The Academy Players Directory*, those agents may then electronically transmit to casting directors the names of talent they would like to see considered for the roles described in the breakdowns. As the incoming e-mail-like transmission links with the casting director's computer, he or she will find the submitted actor's photo and résumé. In the past, this process required the physical delivery of paper and photos, using messengers and taking several hours. This free service provided by *The Academy Players Directory* (to all actors listed in the directory) allows agents to submit actors to casting directors electronically. See chapter 14 for contact information.

### The Players Guide

*The Players Guide* is used throughout the world to contact, locate, and discover talent for stage, screen, radio, and television. It is published just once a year; listings are open to all members of Actors Equity, AFTRA, or SAG. It currently has twenty thousand subscribers. For a $100-per-year fee, actors are included in the directory and entered onto Players Guide CD (CD-ROM) and onto Players Guide on the Web (Internet).

*The Players Guide* is now published in association with *The Spotlight*, a catalog that has served the British entertainment industry for seventy years and maintains the largest database of professional actors in the world.

You can receive an application form by contacting: *The Players Guide,* 1560 Broadway, Suite 416, New York, NY 10036, or call Catherine Lamm at (212) 302 -9474. The deadline for *The Players Guide* is generally late September.

# Networking

**O**ne of the earliest uses of the word "network" dates back to the sixteenth century. Then, it referred to the use of fishing nets. Perhaps the best way to define the word is as "a group you know or can get to know for the purpose of sharing information." It's both a technique and a process centered on specific goals.

### What Is Networking?

Networking is basically a social activity. You purposefully develop relations with others, acquire advice, and exchange information. The most successful type of networking is usually done in person, but the phone and mail are often (especially in cities like New York and Los Angeles) ways to maintain your contacts.

Networking is very much an assertive process. Networkers introduce themselves to others, telephone contacts that they've made (on a regular basis), write notes, make dates, and basically try to always keep in touch.

The idea in networking of "using" people can be a difficult concept to accept for a lot of people. Beginning a relationship with other people not because we like them, but because they may be useful to us may seem manipulative and somewhat crass. But, you must remember, networking is a two-way street. Not only do you receive information from your contacts, you must always be willing to give information when needed. The actor who simply uses people for personal gain and information will come across as insincere, manipulative, and untrustworthy.

In an industry such as show business where there is constant job activity, actors need to know what's happening on a day-to-day basis. Needless to say, networking is a powerful tool for the actor.

### Where to Network

There are networking opportunities for actors almost anywhere that people in the entertainment industry gather. You can network at casting seminars, at auditions, in classes, at the theater, while in rehearsal for a play, at social entertainment gatherings, at theater fund-raisers, on a movie set, or while working on a soap opera. There are many actor support groups that offer excellent networking opportunities. If you can't find one, start one.

### Who to Network With

Almost anyone can be a source of information, from friends to family members to people you meet at a party. The strongest contacts are usually people who work specifically in the industry. Actors often make the mistake of only networking with other actors. You must remember that networking is about gathering all kinds of industry information. Only networking with actors limits the type of information you'll receive. Writers, designers, producers, movie hairstylists, makeup people, etc., are all valid sources of information.

### Know What You Want

Before you actively start networking, it's very important that your career goals be clear. The more specific you are as to what you want and how soon you plan on ascertaining your goal, the better your chances of developing successful networking sources. Be realistic.

Don't be too easy; challenge yourself. Setting specific goals can be very difficult in a field like show business, because there are so many contributing factors to finding work. Actors must realize, however, that they are not helpless victims whose careers are totally dependent on casting directors and agents.

### Skills Necessary to Network

Networking isn't just overhearing other people's tips and secretly storing them away for your own private use. As I've mentioned it's a give-and-take situation that requires specific people skills. These skills include:

- *Being committed.* First and foremost, you must be willing to devote both time and energy to networking. It's a long-term, ongoing process. You must be willing to pursue and maintain relationships with your contacts. Maintaining relationships does not mean only checking in with them when you need something. The communication must be constant, on a regular basis.
- *Showing interest in (empowering) others.* An effective networker shows a genuine interest in the people she's talking to. People need to feel that they are of value. One way to empower someone is simply to listen to them. A by-product of empowering others is that they are much more likely to help you, offer advice, and share potential casting tips.
- *Presenting yourself in a positive, attractive, and knowledgeable manner.* We're all shy to some degree. A good networker must be assertive. Try to look your best and always put your best foot forward in networking situations. Work on your confidence, especially in social situations. One thing you may want to practice at home is a very brief introduction of yourself that you can use in any and all networking situations. First impressions are very important, especially in show business. You want to come across as open, friendly, and available to make new friends.

    You must be willing to share pertinent information that could be of value to others. Let's say you hear of a movie coming into town that might be looking for an extra hairstylist.

One of the contacts you've made is a hairstylist. It behooves you to call that person and let her know. Sharing information is essential to networking. Be generous.

- *Knowing how to ask good questions.* Perhaps one of the strongest networking skills you must develop is the ability to ask the right questions. You must be specific, articulate, and to the point. Use questions that start with "when," "who," "where," and "what" when you need factual information.

- *Being a good listener.* Much of good networking is just plain, good listening. This means not just listening with your ears but also with your eyes. It means being able to look at the speaker, observe his body language, and being able to see what he's really saying. You'd be amazed at how few people know how to really listen. Many actors have a tendency to be self-absorbed, constantly worrying what others are thinking about them. Networking is about open communication with others.

  While in conversation with someone, give the speaker feedback through such things as eye contact, a nod, a smile, or a good question in response to what has just been said.

- *Asking for help.* Whether it's asking other actors (in your network) if they know who'll be casting such-and-such a movie, or just asking another contact for some advice or an opinion, you must be willing to ask others for their assistance. Ask for what you want and try not to be shy about it. If you've developed solid networking relationships with others, asking them for help on occasion is totally appropriate (and necessary).

- *Being able to share your successes.* Keeping the people in your network informed about your achievements is a vital aspect of successful networking. Many actors feel quite comfortable complaining about the slumps in their careers, but are reticent about sharing their successes. Sharing your success doesn't mean being pompous, nor does it mean being falsely humble. Just be proud of yourself. If you auditioned for a job and got the role, share it with your network. Your sharing may be just the right impetus that another actor needs to be inspired to get out of a slump she's in.

- *Being ready and willing to follow up.* If you say you're going to do something, then do it. How often have you said to someone,

"I'll give you a call" or "Let's have lunch next week," and never followed through? When it comes to successful networking, you must keep your word. Aside from showing that you're serious about the business, it also shows that you're dependable.

### Networking at Social and Business Events

When going to social or business events, you should decide beforehand what networking goals you'd like to accomplish. Know as much as you can about the event. Who will be there? What is the purpose of the event? Try to look your best. Bring a pen and pad and some business cards. If it's appropriate, bring some eight-by-tens. The basic idea at these events is not to make a lot of contacts but, with luck, to make some strong ones (even if it's only one or two).

- *Entering the room.* When you enter the room, stand in the doorway for a moment. This is a time to get yourself centered and see what's going on. See who's there, who you know, who you want to know. Feel the energy in the room. Is it noisy? Calm? Is there a lot of activity? For some reason, the corners of the room are usually the places where the power groups form. Decide which people you'd like to meet and then go over to them.

- *Making the initial contact.* Making contact for the first time is the most difficult part of networking for a lot of people. It requires being assertive. Smile, introduce yourself, make eye contact, and shake the hand of the person you've said hello to. Don't shake her hand too tensely or too passively. Just a good, warm, friendly handshake.

- *What to say.* After saying hello and shaking hands, you can discuss the event. If you've introduced yourself to someone whose work you're familiar with, let him know. Be genuinely complimentary if you can. If he's an actor you've recently seen in a play or movie and you enjoyed his work, let him know. Start a conversation. Ask questions and listen to what he has to say. Notice if he seems comfortable talking with you. If it's someone you feel you'd like to maintain contact with, feel free to give him your card and/or ask him for his number. Try not to spend too much time with any one person at social events. Tell him you'll give him a call, say good-bye, and circulate. You might want to jot down any pertinent information on the back of his business card when you have a chance.

- *Dealing with people you don't want to talk to.* At all social events there are always going to be people who will approach you who (for whatever reason) you don't care to talk to. Wasting time in conversation with them is exactly that—wasting time. The secret is simply to break off the conversation with them politely with one of several phrases. You can try, "It was great meeting you, hope to see you again." Or, "I'd really like to continue talking with you, but there are so many people I promised to say hello to." Smile, say good-bye, then quickly go over to someone else and say hello.

- *Talking to casting directors and talent agents.* With casting directors and agents, the rules at social events are a bit different. If at an event there is a casting director or agent you'd like to meet, certainly feel free to do so. It's important, however, to sense if, when you introduce yourself to her, she is open to chatting with you. If you sense she's not, don't wear out your welcome. Just say, "My name is. . . . I just came over to say hi." Then subtly, politely move on.

  If you feel she is open to meeting you, you can start off by discussing the event. If you've recently seen a film that she cast, you may want to compliment her work, talk about what you liked about the project. If you want, you can talk about yourself. But don't verbalize your résumé! That is, don't stand there listing everything you've been doing professionally for the last few years. That is a bore! Actors do it all the time at social events. I'm sure it comes out of nerves, but it's very unappealing. If she asks you specifically what you've been doing lately, feel free to tell her, but be succinct. Also, remember that casting directors and agents are human beings. You should relate to them with the same social respect you would anyone else. Actors who come across as blatant self-promoters, boasting about their work in this film or that can be annoying and obnoxious. Above all, always try to present yourself as a professional. You certainly don't want to come across as negative or unlikeable. Putting down the director or producer of a project on which you worked is not smart; neither is complaining. Try to be positive and open.

### The Follow-Up

Once you've made the initial contact, the follow-up is one of the most important aspects of the networking process. Maintaining communication with your contacts is vital to successful networking.

### After the Initial Contact: Actors, Directors, Designers

A day or two after the event you should contact the actors with whom you exchanged cards (unless they call you first). The call should be friendly, letting them know how much you enjoyed meeting them. Perhaps you can suggest getting together for coffee, lunch, or going to the theater together. Always keep the focus friendly and business oriented. If they seem receptive, make the arrangements. If they seem somewhat reluctant or offer a lot of excuses, then politely suggest that they call you when they have a chance.

Another way of maintaining contact with people you've met is to support their work. Show up at the theater when you've found out they're involved in a play or a reading. Supporting each other through work is a strong way to develop networking circles.

If you hear of a role being cast that one of the actors in your networking group might be right for, give her a call, let her know. If you know of a show looking for a set designer and you know one, give him a call. Be giving. What goes around, comes around.

### After the Initial Contact: Casting Directors, Talent Agents

Unless they specifically suggested that you call their offices, most casting directors and talent agents prefer not to get unsolicited phone calls. A friendly note (with a picture and résumé attached) telling them how nice it was meeting them at the event is always a good idea. In your note, don't forget to remind them where and when it was that you met. Also, it helps if you can refer to anything that you discussed (they may have met a lot of people that night). Make the note polite, cordial, and brief. Tell them you'd like to keep them posted about events going on in your career. Mention that you hope they'll keep you in mind for anything that they feel you're right for in the future. Keep your word; put them on your contact list and keep them posted.

Generally, the frequency and type of contact with casting directors and talent agents will be different than with most of your networking contacts. It's a bit more businesslike, less social (usually), and more specifically work oriented.

### Sustaining Your Networks

"Keeping in touch" with the contacts you've made is vital to sustaining networks. How often, how well you know them, how strong the contact is, whether you speak only on the phone, etc., are factors that determine how you keep in touch. Some contacts like to be very social while others prefer only a brief phone call now and then.

### Lunches and Get-Togethers: Expanding Your Network

Some actors create networking meetings on a weekly or monthly basis to share information and to offer support to other members. Socializing is another way to develop your networks. Inviting several of your contacts for lunch or having a party is a pleasant way to meet in groups. When people meet in small social circles, they are more relaxed, more accessible. And as you invite your contacts to social gatherings, hopefully they'll invite you to theirs. This is often how you meet more contacts and expand your network.

Whether you should invite casting directors and talent agents to your networking social functions is a hard call. It has to do with the nature of your relationships with them and the appropriateness of the occasion. Be sensitive as to how they'd feel at such an event (and how you'd feel having them there).

# Promoting Your Career on the Internet

In the not too distant future, the Internet may become a great source of casting opportunities for actors. At present, however, even though the technology is available, all the kinks of online casting have yet to be worked out. My advice to actors who are thinking of listing themselves with some of the many fee-charging casting services is to hold off until you've carefully researched their validity. One thing you'll soon discover is that quite a few of these companies are fly-by-night, rip-off artists. That's certainly not to say that there aren't several reputable online companies offering valuable services to their actor clients.

There are certain things to look for before signing up with any online casting company:

- Find out how long the service has been in operation.
- Ask around—find out what kind of reputation the company has (ask other actors who may have dealt with them).
- If the company charges a fee, find out exactly what you get for your money.
- Ask how many actor-clients it presently has.
- Find out how actors are contacted. If an interested director can

only contact you by e-mail or through an agent and you don't have either, what's the point?

- See if any other theater websites validate the company's services (by listing it as a contact).
- Find out where it's located (a mailing address), telephone number, etc.
- When talking with the company, try to get a sense of how well organized it is, how legit, how well informed about the business, etc.
- Find out how often its website is hit.

### Pros and Cons

I know of many actors who have gotten work in industrials, showcases, low-budget independent films, and as extras by e-mailing their photos to contacts made from website bulletin boards.

However, the casting directors that I spoke with, for the most part, felt that online casting had a limited potential. Karen Kayser, at Steve and Linda Horn Casting, felt that at present "they're not of much value, and most of them are a rip-off."

Several other casting directors (who didn't want to be quoted) felt similarly to Kayser, saying that "subjectivity" was one of the main components in casting, and that no online computer service could "feel" (yet).

Another thing to consider is that many of these online casting companies were started by computer businesspeople who are not very savvy about the entertainment industry. Younger, less experienced actors are certainly key targets for many of the companies.

Online casting services are particularly good for networking. Meeting other actors online and sharing information is always useful. According to Buzz Communication (see listings below), "The Web is a great supplement to an actor's marketing tools. It reaches agents and casting directors the actor wouldn't normally be in contact with, including those out of town, new/one-time productions, and areas the actor isn't focusing on (print, voice-overs, commercials, trade shows). In addition, the Web makes their headshots available twenty-four hours a day, around the globe."

### Some Online Suggestions

After researching many of the websites, I decided to list a few of them. My recommendations are based primarily on my own personal investigation, the site's reputation, and simple word of mouth. This is by no means a complete list. There are many other dependable sites.

### Playbill Online

Contact: America Online members can use the keyword "Playbill." Web surfers search for "Playbill," or "Theater Central." The website was launched June 2, 1995, and it is described as "a place where members can get information about the world of theater. They can participate in chats with artists, write them messages on the message boards, make contacts, and even find a job."

In the Industry section, there is access to fourteen message boards and live chats, hundreds of job postings, newsletters from a variety of theater organizations, and a database of college programs. In the Multimedia section, you can browse through theater books, CD-ROMs, videos, scripts, audio clips, and theater art. *Playbill*'s Features section lists theater profiles, and interviews, and present trends are provided along with information about theater awards, "Who's Who," photos, travel information, casting calls, and much more.

### The Academy Players Directory (The Link)

Contact: *The Academy Players Directory* online can be reached via e-mail at *ampas@ampas.org.* For the mailing address and telephone number see page 79.

This service, provided by *The Academy Players Directory* and Breakdown Services, Ltd., streamlines the photo-submission process between talent agents and casting directors. Breakdown Services electronically transmits its daily breakdowns of available acting roles to its agent clients. Using the CD-ROM version of *The Academy Players Directory* (called PD-ROM), casting directors will find the submitted actor's photo, credits, attributes, and skills on their computer monitors.

The Link currently has more than 16,000 listings of union talent in its database, and expects this number to increase dramatically once its automated system takes off. (For further information on this service, see chapter 12.)

### The Players Guide (in association with The Spotlight)

Contact: *The Players Guide* can be reached via e-mail at *info@ players-guide.com*. For the mailing address and telephone number, see page 78.

The Spotlight has more than 25,000 listings. A special feature that it offers is an infinite number of informational fields that a casting director can initiate to search for individual talent. It also offers a "notebooking feature" that allows casting agents to take notes on individual talent, which is stored on the hard drive to be recalled year after year. Within the next several years the company will be offering audio- and visual tapes.

### Buzz Communication

Contact: On the Web, go to BuzzNYC (*www.buzznyc.com*) or BuzzLA (*buzzla.com*). You may also call (212) 353-2800 or fax (212) 353-3211.

Buzz Communication presently lists about four hundred actors on its site. The headshots are digitally scanned for display on the site, and résumés are inputted in a database and formatted for display online.

According to Buzz, "A casting director, agent, filmmaker, or producer can find talent in a variety of ways: he/she can sort the résumés based on union status, age, range, ethnicity, sex, etc., find an actor by name, or just look at everybody. He/she can also search the résumés for keywords, such as a specific role or skill."

The site is accessed more than ten thousand times every day. Most of the people using the Buzz database are independent filmmakers and regional theater producers.

### Scott's Theater-Link.Com

Contact: On the Web, go to *www.theatre.link.com*.

Scott's is a casting and contact service, offering several listings. Among the services it offers are: Act Now, which brings talent and casting together; Internet Stage and Screen Resources, a production source; Talent Network, which provides a service directory; and Theater People, a casting and contact service.

### Iam Magazine

Contact: *Iam* Magazine, P.O. Box 523, Melbourne, FL 32902-0523; (407) 773-3615, fax (407) 773-9951; e-mail *iam@mail.wwinternet.net.*

*Iam* reports on funding and career opportunities in motion pictures, television, recording, and theater. It also lists feature films in preparation and preproduction, and offers a complete list of shows on prime-time networks. It also lists comprehensive, up-to-date casting information as well as articles on the business of entertainment.

# *Casting Seminars*

$(212)$ $977-6666$

**W**hat are casting seminars? According to Bunny Levine, co-owner of The Actors Connection, a casting seminar company in New York, "They are extraordinary opportunities to meet industry guests, learn about them as people and about their offices, and show them a bit of your work."

Casting directors and agents meet with actors at these seminars and either listen to a prepared monologue, a cold reading of a scene or commercial copy, or listen to the actor sing. According to Levine, "Sometimes positive results are immediate; occasionally actors report auditions and bookings as much as a year after meeting a guest. And sometimes a meeting is simply a foot in the door, a first meeting that should be followed up periodically with correspondence and subsequent seminars. Or, at the very least, it enables you to invite guests to your next performance, with some assurance that they'll recognize your name and face." Levine also says that the seminars "provide great networking opportunities with fellow actors." She does stress, however, that "meeting a guest is never a guarantee of employment."

Alan Nusbaum, who owns Talent Ventures Incorporated acting schools, which include casting seminars as part of their curriculum, says his casting seminars give actors "a great opportunity to get specific feedback on their work from working professionals. The idea of getting your work critiqued directly by casting directors can be very helpful and insightful to the actor who's ready to have his work seen professionally."

### At the Seminars: What Happens?

Most of the seminars begin with a question-and-answer period with the guest for a half hour to forty-five minutes. The idea here is for the actors to find out about how the guest's office works. It's a time for the actors to get a sense of the guest, her likes, dislikes, and specifically what her office is all about. Then, after a short break, the actors perform their prepared work or do cold readings. Generally, actors are allowed three minutes to perform a monologue (or songs or a combination thereof), or six-and-a-half minutes for a prepared scene.

Next, the casting director gives the actors feedback on what she saw. The emphasis here should be on learning, not auditioning.

Actors should not react emotionally to the casting director's criticisms, just take them in. If you're unclear about what the casting director meant, you should certainly ask for clarification. Another, less common, format, is one in which the guest sees the actor for a six- to ten-minute one-on-one interview (and then sees the actor's work).

One of the benefits of these seminars is that you get to see the casting directors and agents as human beings, not as some powerful, godlike entity who can make or break your career.

### Protocol and Courtesy at the Seminar

There are certain courtesies expected from actors at the seminars. According to Bunny Levine, actors should "arrive on time and stay until the end of the seminar. You'd be surprised at how much you can learn from what the guest says to the other actors and also how important your presence and support are to the others." Levine says that many of the guests (the casting directors or agents) resent early departures. Also, she says, "This should be an environment of support for each other, not of competitiveness. On the rare occasion that an actor does not perform to our standards, we consult and advise him or her about classes and other ways to achieve the level of performance."

Try to learn from the casting director's comments on your work: "Don't complain. Don't explain."

### Interviews with Casting Seminar Owners

BUNNY LEVINE (**BL**) is co-owner with her husband Bernie of the Actors Connection, a successful casting seminar company located in New York City that has been in existence for over nine years.

ALAN NUSBAUM (**AN**) is CEO and founder of TVI (Talent Ventures Incorporated), one of the largest acting schools, with offices in New York City and Miami, and its headquarters in Los Angeles. He is planning to open other schools in Chicago, Orlando, and London.

---

**At what point in their careers should actors begin taking casting seminars?**

**BL:** When they're truly ready to put themselves out as professionals. I feel that they should have studied a minimum of two years part time or at least one year in a full-time program at one of the reputable schools.

**AN:** When they have a good foundation of the fundamentals of acting. When they feel confident about themselves and their work. And when the actor has work that he's confident about showing.

**What are the most common mistakes actors make at these seminars? How can they avoid them?**

**BL:** Many actors think that their careers depend on them getting a legit agent. We feel that that's probably the last thing that happens for most actors. First, actors should establish contacts with casting directors and commercial agents and "extras" casting directors. Actors should build a dossier of their work that they can put on their résumés. Under-fives (parts with five lines and under), day players, small commercials, a role in an independent film, are all résumé builders. When actors meet legit agents before they have any work of substance and nothing much happens from that meeting, they're disappointed. The actor is prone to blame us rather than to take responsibility and realize that there really is an order to things.

At the seminars, actors who come across as confrontational, hostile, or negative will rarely find anyone who wants to work with them. Being aggressive, too overconfident, asking twenty questions rather than just one good one, and coming before their work is ready to be seen are all ways actors do themselves a disservice in these seminars.

**AN:** They come into the seminars seeking employment instead of coming to learn from the casting director or agent. They come across as too desperate. If the actor is confident in his talent, he shouldn't have any difficulty accepting what the guest has to say, to learn from the comments, and to be able to utilize them. The confident actor won't be so preoccupied with making an impression.

Another mistake that actors make at these seminars is they come unprepared. They forget their pictures and résumés, or sometimes something as little as not having the picture stapled to the résumé.

### What type of prepared material should actors select for these seminars?

**BL:** For the most part, agents and casting directors ask for contemporary material that isn't overdone. Also keep it on the lighter side. Remember, it's the end of the agent's long day, you don't want to have too many heavy monologues. If, however, you're more adept at heavier, more dramatic material, then certainly you should do it.

For musical auditions you should sing songs of Broadway caliber.

**AN:** Something light and comedic that hasn't been done a hundred times before. Make the monologues contemporary. It doesn't make too much of a difference if it's comedic or dramatic, as long as you have your moment in the monologue. When you do a comic piece that makes people laugh, they tend to remember you more. With scenes, problems come up when the scene is too long or when the actor "over-props" it and it becomes a scene about props.

**What types of mistakes do actors make when doing cold readings at these seminars?**

**BL:** Doing cold reading is really an art that can be developed. You must practice doing cold readings before taking a seminar that requires one. The most common cold reading mistakes are not making eye contact, not making strong choices.

**AN:** Not listening to his partner. The actor has an agenda going. He doesn't respond to what's being given to him by the other person.

**What is considered appropriate/inappropriate behavior at these seminars between the actor and the guest?**

**BL:** They shouldn't schmooze with the casting director or agent. Also, you shouldn't get too personal. Don't tell the casting director that you've been writing to her office for seven years and have never gotten a reply. The casting seminar is not the place to bring this up. Good questions are, What types do you use? Do you use all ethnicities? and Do you use all ages? Don't ask questions that are abrasive or confrontational.

**AN:** Respect the person's position. Always show up early for these seminars. The actor should not approach the casting director and ask, Are you currently looking for such-and-such? Questions that come down to, Are you going to hire me? Are you going to bring me in for this role? Are you going to represent me or freelance with me? are not really even self-serving, they're just stupid and counterproductive.

**What factors should actors keep in mind when selecting guests?**

**BL:** Be realistic. A beginning actor should target the good but medium-sized agent. Consult with us at The Actors Connection letting us know specifically what your goals are.

**AN:** Go to a variety of casting director seminars. You can gain some value from the variety of casting directors' responses. Actors should do some research before making any selections. For instance, if the actor is just starting out and doesn't have too much experience, he might want to take a seminar with a smaller agency that could be more open to him.

# Talent Tours

**T**alent tours are junkets with groups of actors that go to specific cities where actors are likely to find substantial work opportunities. There they meet with and showcase their talent for casting directors and agents who work predominantly in that area. They are geared for the actor who is of one of two minds: First, the actor who has decided to move there and wants to get all the information he can before going; or second, the actor who is seriously considering moving but before making the trip "cold turkey" wants something to base the move on. During these junkets the actors get an opportunity to network with people who are players within the industry. They get to experience how the business is different in that city. Junkets go to New York City, Los Angeles, Chicago, and sometimes other cities. Some of these seminars also include meetings with local photographers and real estate agents who can help actors with housing. One thing that actors should realize is that these tours should not be thought of as a vacation.

### Interviews with Talent Tour Operators

BUNNY LEVINE (**BL**) is co-owner of The Actors Connection, a nine-year-old company that arranges travel tours for actors.

ALAN NUSBAUM (**AN**) is CEO and founder of TVI (Talent Ventures Incorporated), a company that arranges travel tours for actors.

---

### Why and when should an actor take a talent tour?

**BL:** It's for actors who aren't sure if they're ready to make the move to these cities, or for actors who are definitely planning on moving there. Travel tours serve both of their agendas.

**AN:** When an actor is considering moving to Los Angeles in the next twenty-four months, this is a great opportunity to check it out. He or she can see what it's like before moving out there. Travel tours also provide the actor with contacts when he or she does move out there. Aside from finding out where to live, the actors also get to know different agents and casting directors and get a sense of what they expect of actors.

### What occurs on these tours on a day-to-day basis?

**BL:** We have a three-hour orientation session on the day they get there given by an actor who previously lived in New York and now has moved to Los Angeles. Then, starting the next morning there's a 10:00 A.M. seminar, a 2:00 P.M. seminar, and a 7:00 P.M. seminar. There is one day off during the tour for rest and relaxation (midway through). The tour is over five days later.

**AN:** We usually do these tours five times a year. There's usually twenty-four actors in each group (usually two groups go out there at the same time). They usually start at ten in the morning. The majority of actors stay at a hotel that we arrange for them that's only a mile from our studio in Los Angeles. There are five or six sessions a day. Each session begins with a question-and-answer period where the actors can learn about the casting director, her office, and what she casts. Then the casting director hands out scenes and works with each actor individually. Next, the actors are critiqued and get feedback on their work.

### What should/shouldn't an actor expect from these tours?

**BL:** You shouldn't expect immediate success. Ironically, if you're a good New York type, with good credits, you have a better chance of being signed in L.A. than in New York. Results can also be quicker if you're a well-trained New York actor. Training means a lot to some of the casting directors. Also, the volume is so much more enormous out there, so the results can be more immediate.

**AN:** You shouldn't expect to be signed on the spot. If you're what they're looking for, they have your résumé. You have to learn to be patient. You can get a point of view on your work that might vary a bit from the New York casting directors. The needs in Los Angeles are different than in New York. Being a New York actor with substantial theater credits is always a plus out there.

### What do actors need to prepare for these tours?

**BL:** They need to be good at cold readings. They hardly use monologues in Los Angeles. They hand out scenes from movies and TV for you to read cold. Actors should be aware of the Los Angeles weather and mode and bring along an appropriate wardrobe.

**AN:** Two monologues, casual clothing, lots of pictures and résumés, and that's about it.

# *Talent Agents*

**A**gents do not get you jobs. Despite what many actors believe, only you can get yourself an acting job (usually through an audition). Agents may recommend you for a job. They submit your picture and résumé to casting directors. They can set up appointments, interviews, and auditions for you. And, occasionally, they can give you some career guidance.

It has been said many times: the talent agent is the seller in the equation, the casting director is the buyer, and you, the actor, are the product. Simplistic, perhaps a bit coarse, but bottom line—show business is a business.

Most agents are franchised (licensed) by all of the actors' unions (Actors Equity Association, SAG, and AFTRA). In Los Angeles, many agents don't have Actors Equity franchising as theater and quite often it is not a medium that they choose to work in. It is to your advantage as an actor to work with franchised agents only. By law, they must follow certain ethical and professional standards. You may do this, by the way, even if you yourself are not a member of any of the three unions that franchise agents. Union actors can only work with agents that are franchised in their particular affiliations.

### Commissions

Talent agents receive a 10 percent commission for their services. The 10 percent commission that they are entitled to is paid only after you are paid, never before. There are some stories of unscrupulous agents who ask for their commissions in advance. This is not the way it works.

### Freelance versus Signed

There are two ways an actor can work with an agent—freelance or signed. When an actor freelances with one agency, he has the right to freelance with other agencies. That is, there is no exclusivity to the professional commitment; other agents may also send him out on auditions.

A "signed client agreement" occurs when an agency and an actor have agreed to work exclusively with each other (either in a particular area or in all three areas). The actor cannot freelance with any other agency in the field(s) that the contract covers.

There are agencies that handle only freelance clients as there are signed-client-only agencies. A third type of agency handles both freelance and signed clients. In this case, the agencies try to find work for their signed clients first. Beneath the signed clients on the totem pole are the freelance clients whom the agent calls when none of his signed clients fill the bill for a particular job.

### When to Seek Representation

Jonn Wasser, one of the talent agents that I interviewed (see chapter 18), said, "Agents are looking for actors who aren't looking for agents. Agents are looking for actors that are going places." Perhaps one of the biggest turnoffs to most talent agents is meeting desperate actors who believe that they can't have any kind of a career without an agent. That desperation permeates their interviews and sometimes their work. There's no question that in Los Angeles you need representation to get most work.

Actors living and working in New York City, however, can fend for themselves to some degree without an agent. As an actor with whom I recently spoke said, "Life without an agent in New York is definitely do-able."

Before seeking representation, make sure that you're really ready. Being ready means having enough training under your belt. You must feel confident about yourself and your talent. You must be able to present yourself as personable and professional. The agent must believe in you and must feel passionate about your talent.

Experience is another factor that agents consider before signing an actor. The more professional theater, film, and television experience you have, the better.

If you're just out of school, try to get into some acting showcases, some independent and student films. Do some extra work and under-five work on soaps. Get your face seen, build up your résumé.

For those actors who are more experienced (and have signed with talent agents previously), the questions for both the actor and the prospective agent are, What can the agent do to move the actor's career to the next level? and, What can be done that hasn't been done previously?

Both experienced and inexperienced actors need to research the agents they're interested in. You might want to know which actors they work with (their client lists). You may be too similar to some of their existing clients. Are they the right-sized agency for you? They could be too big (you could get lost in the shuffle) or not big enough (when you're better connected with casting directors than they are).

It's also important to find out about the other agents at the agency with which you are considering working. How long have they been with this agency? What are their backgrounds? Would you feel confident with them representing you? Negotiating for you? Do they see you the way you see yourself (type- and talentwise)? These questions are just a few of the many that you should consider before signing with any agent. Remember, signing with an agent is a commitment. You are putting your trust and your future in his or her hands.

# Interviews with Talent Agents

**R**ICHARD BAUMAN (**RB**) is an agent with Bauman Hiller and Associates, in its Los Angeles office. The agency handles talent for film, TV, and theater. Bauman opened his first office in New York City in 1963. Presently, he represents or has represented Sada Thompson, Nancy Marchand, Moses Gun, and Robert De Niro.

MARTIN GAGE (**MG**), of the Martin Gage Agency in Los Angeles, handles talent for film, TV, and theater. He has been an agent for thirty-six years. His agency opened its New York City office in 1973 and its West Coast office in 1975. He presently represents or has represented Robert Pastorelli, Geraldine Page, Kim Basinger, Woody Harrelson, and Bernadette Peters.

HOLLY LEAVITT (**HL**) is with J. Michael Bloom in Los Angeles. (There is also an East Coast office.) The agency handles talent for film, TV, theater, and commercials. The commercial department in New York is quite strong. Leavitt got her training working with Lucy Kroll in New York for ten years. Leavitt worked with such actors as Uta Hagen, Fritz Weaver, and James Earl Jones.

JONN WASSER (**JW**) has been with Don Buchwald and Associates, New York (there is also a Los Angeles office), for eight years. He is head of the promo department. Prior to joining the agency, he was head of the Corporate Sponsorship Program at Radio City Music Hall.

MARK REDANTY (**MR**), of Bauman Hiller and Associates' New York City office, has been an agent since 1984. He represents or has represented Robert Morse, Donna McKechnie, Scott Wise, and Jodi Benson.

SUSAN SMITH (**SS**) is with Susan Smith and Associates in Los Angeles. The agency has been in business for almost twenty-eight years.

---

### How would you describe your job?

**RB:** It's quite different than it was thirty years ago. Then we took great pride in developing talent from an unknown stage to hopefully becoming a star. Now, particularly in Hollywood, it's very difficult. What agents do is try to get their actors seen by the casting people or producers or directors. A lot of the people [casting directors] with whom you deal don't know many of the people [actors] you're talking about. It can sometimes be quite frustrating, really. We try to get our actors auditions, and if they get the job, we negotiate salaries and contracts.

**RB:** My job is twofold: to get jobs for people and to negotiate contracts, and to guide careers. Part of my job is also managerial, that is, I also do what some managers do.

**HL:** It's really a combination of salesperson, psychologist, baby-sitter, lawyer, and dreamer.

**JW:** Basically, I'm a salesman. I sell talent. We're licensed by the city of New York as an employment agency. I seek out opportunities for clients, primarily now in the broadcast-promotional field. For instance, you'll hear on TV, "Coming up on channel 4 Glen Smith talks about so-and-so." That's called a promo, which is one type of voice-over that's highly competitive but is also highly lucrative. One of the actors we represent used to be in the chorus of *Les Misérables* and now he does a lot of work for HBO. His income has increased dramatically.

**MR:** My definition of an agent comes from the play *End of the World* by Arthur Kopit. In it there's an agent who says, "An agent's function is to field offers for her clients." I try to help my clients get work and then negotiate their contracts.

**SS:** What I do is find work for actors. Talent agencies are really employment agencies for actors. I also guide actors' careers and help with decisions in career planning.

### How and where do you find the actors you work with?

**RB:** Usually by referral. Sometimes from a cassette they've sent. I've gotten quite a few actors from Equity waiver plays. Sometimes you see them in a marvelous role on television and find out who they are and if they're represented. If they're not, you contact them and have them come in.

**RB:** I find them all over. I used to find them at schools. I found Tim Robbins at UCLA. I've found a lot of actors in showcases. But I can tell you that you can see five hundred actors before you sign one. My agents go to see everything and we watch television. The advent of the videotapes has been extremely helpful for us in finding new talent.

**HL:** Any way we can. From recommendations to finding them at showcases or in a film or on a videotape that they've sent.

**JW:** Referrals, showcases, voice-over tapes. Just to mention it, the voice-over tapes have to be perfect. Otherwise, it's a waste of time. We scout comedy clubs a lot.

**MR:** I interview at least one actor every day in my office. I meet many of them through referrals. Also, I give seminars on "How to Get Your Career Started" at schools all around the country. I've met clients there while they're still in school. I'll go to schools such as Boston University, University of Utah, and North Carolina School of the Arts.

**SS:** In the beginning I used to go to every basement and attic to find talent. Today, the way the agency is, it's primarily through recommendation and also at the drama schools.

**What types of things do you look for in a headshot? On a résumé? On a videotape?**

**RB:** I look to see if the person would look like that because most actors select a picture that doesn't look like them. What they usually select are the photos of how they think they'd like to look. My advice is take the pictures outside in a natural light.

On the résumé what I look for is the truth. So often I notice that actors put down things that I know they haven't done. Or I'll notice that they're presently taking eight different kinds of classes. Nobody needs to take eight different kinds of classes. I look to see if what they do is representative of what they want to do.

On the videotapes you get a sense of how they look. Can they walk across a room? What their concentration is like, their vocal quality, things like that.

**MG:** Headshots must look like the person. I'm an eye person, so I look to their eyes in their photos. We sometimes get forty photos a day. It's rare we call in someone just from the photo, but if the face has something really extraordinary going on. . . .

On the résumé you want strong credits, but I'll tell you I've taken people who have had no credits, right out of the schools. When someone lies on his résumé, it's very annoying. But everyone does it. I used to do it when I was a young actor. But it doesn't pay. You get caught. When I see a credit for a show that I saw, I know whether or not they were in it. And I can easily find out. I have almost every playbill of every play I've seen since 1950, and I have notes. So I go home and check on it. Or they'll say they were directed by so-and-so, and that director's a friend of mine. A phone call later and the truth comes out. It's very simple to check on someone's credit.

The videotape has become very important. When you don't know someone's work firsthand, that videotape is like gold. Basic acting skills are immediately apparent. Presence is obvious. I won't look at a poorly made tape. It must be a professional tape with professional jobs that you've done. Six minutes at most. One good scene can tell me all about you, but two or three is preferable. And it shouldn't be a scene where there are five guys sitting around a table talking and all of a sudden you come running in with your two lines. The most important thing for an agent is that he knows what to do with you, how he can best sell you. The videotape must offer him some clue. If you don't know who that actor is and what they do, then how can you sell them? I've had actors, especially New York actors who say, "Just take a chance and send me out."

I have a reputation too. This issue is really a problem. You must know what you can do, how you can best sell the actor.

**HL:** It's the essence of the person. I want the picture not to look too retouched. Like everyone else, I look at the eyes. I like the body shots. On the résumé I want to see if the person has a well-rounded career. Is it legible? Are the spellings of names and theaters correct? A lot of misspellings on a résumé tells me something about the actor. Who they've studied with is important to me. The videotape can really let me know a great deal about the actor. It's a walking, talking audition except that it's finished work. The choice of the material is also important to me. Things like *America's Most Wanted* are so cheesy. Unless you have a really great scene from that show, it's not the best one to include. Keep the tapes from six to eight minutes. If you've got really great material, it can be a bit longer.

**JW:** Since I still work on a lot of on-camera commercials all of those apply to me. On the headshot, the personality must pop out. Obviously, good looks count first. It's like a blind date. The good-looking person will get through the door easier. On the résumé misspellings turn me off. Then you know the actor doesn't consider himself a professional. I look for substantial credits unless you're twenty-two and right off the boat. The videotapes help also. Is he mesmerizing on camera? Is there something in his performance that pulls me in? Does his picture match his videotape (which many times it doesn't)?

**MR:** If I'm looking at a picture and the actor is absolutely gorgeous, naturally that'll interest me. But that's not to say that's all I look for.

On the résumé: Good training, good experience based upon age. Number of years in the business.

On the videotape: You assume that the videotape is a good representation of the actor's work and it isn't always. Sometimes the actor has not been given the type of opportunities. I'd rather see what the actor will choose on her own, like a monologue in which the actor is showing you what she considers to be the best of her work. Actors who have been around a while may have a volume of work on their videotapes. Young actors who haven't booked that much yet may be brilliant but they just haven't had the opportunity. I'm a New York agent and I'm very much into theater.

**SS:** I want the headshots to be interesting. I don't like when they're arty. I prefer darker colors in the photos. I certainly don't like "modely" looking photos. Most of my clients are pretty well known, so in many cases I don't have to send their photos over to the casting directors. As for the résumé, I want to see good theater credits. As for a lot of episodic work on TV, don't waste all the space. Just list numerous episodes of such-and-such a show. Never list commercials. As for the videotapes, I'd rather have one good piece than several little snippets from several shows.

### When interviewing actors, what do you look for?

**RB:** I try to find out where they're from, who they are, what they like to do. I don't talk about the business. I try to find out who they are because really that's what it's all about. So many times when someone comes in they're very nervous. You try to make them relax. You make them laugh, put them at ease. If, when they start to hand me their picture and résumé, I notice that their hand is shaking I'll say, "Forget that for a minute. Did you see the hockey game last night?" Something like that. I try to get to see who they are.

**MG:** As I said, do I know what to do with you? Do I want to do it with you? I must like you. I need to believe I'll be able to work with you, that you will be easy to work with, that you will fit into this office. Also, at the interview it's really a waste of time to complain about your former agent and how he "done you wrong." I immediately think that if I work with this actor and it doesn't work out, will he be bad-mouthing me to the next agent?

**HL:** I want to see a human being who breathes and is alive. I don't want to see someone who feels the need to hide. I hate when actors lie to me. It makes me really uncomfortable. I have called actors on it. I just want to get them out of my office.

**JW:** I look for them to run the interview. If I have to pull it out of you, it makes my job very difficult. But if I saw you in a brilliant showcase and I think you're the next Brad Pitt, I don't give a hoot if you sit there and suck your thumb. However, a lot of it is about personality. An actor can do his homework before an interview. It's one thing he can do to prepare. Find out who we represent, a little bit about me. But the bottom line, be yourself. Don't put on any airs. Relax. As crass as this sounds, you must realize that you're a commodity, you're the product. Look around at what people are buying. Seems very basic and crude, but that's it in a nutshell. Market yourself as a product.

**MR:** I try to get the actor to relax and be himself. I need to find out if this is the kind of person I want to work with the rest of my career. I want to see if he has a sense of his ability in relation to the industry. I want to see if he knows what the industry is like. Is he a team player, someone easy to get along with?

**SS:** I look for an intelligent person. Show me a stupid person and I'll show you a stupid actor. Tell me who you are as a human being. I can see all your credits on the résumé, now tell me about you. What's important to you in life? What makes you the person that you are?

**Do you have a specific process, a way of working with the daily breakdowns?**

**RB:** The breakdowns have become a necessity because there aren't just five studios anymore. So you have hundreds of people casting hundreds of things. In the old days, you went around to the studios and spoke to the people eye to eye, trying to get your clients in. Now, many times, when you talk about somebody, ask, "Do you know so-and-so?" She'll say, "Yes, but he's not right." Well she actually doesn't know him. She's saying he's not right because she doesn't want to admit she really doesn't know him. I can tell. It's very annoying. With the episodic breakdowns, I have a staff and they work on those. The rest of us work on movies of the week and series and things. There you usually have a script beforehand and you know what's going to be on the breakdowns. Naturally, every agent feels that they have someone who's right for a great many of the roles. But they're not going to get it, they'll go to stars. They want the show to get the ratings. So you gear it for some of the other roles. Or if someone really is right, you knock down all the doors until nobody else can say no. It can happen.

**MG:** I don't do much of the day-to-day anymore. I handle a lot of the selling of movie scripts in the agency. I do a small amount of the submissions. Certain casting directors are very demanding, and they have a right to be. Generally, I'll work with them personally. They also have known me for a very long time. As for the breakdowns, I always like two views on everything.

**HL:** At Bloom we all go over the breakdowns together. We usually get the scripts in advance and break them down ourselves so that we're always up-to-date. The breakdowns are only one of several tools that we use to decide on which actors would best fit a role.

**JW:** I deal with commercial breakdowns. There might be one a day. Most of what I do is on the phone. For instance, one casting director, casting a Tide commercial for one day, might call five or six agents. They'll call, not put it in a breakdown. We'll get a call for an AT&T commercial. They'll be looking for two businessmen. One in his fifties, a CEO type, one in his thirties, a young executive. The whole process is much quicker. We'll get the call Monday, it casts Tuesday, the callback's Thursday, then it'll shoot the following Monday. The way I decide which actors to send is by being familiar with the types that AT&T has been using most recently in its present spots. Always be aware of the immediacy of a commercial. You just have seconds to catch the viewer's attention and belief. You've got to be right on target in your casting.

**MR:** My associate does them first and then he brings them in to me. Then I add or subtract anyone that I feel he may have overlooked. I tend to oversubmit rather than undersubmit. I'd rather have the casting director say no than not give the actor the opportunity because I didn't submit her. I submit based on age and ability and obviously who's most right for it. The more explicit the breakdown, the more you can do. What I don't like is when you have a breakdown that doesn't have any ages delineated. I generally use the breakdown as the main information first, then I look at the script, which I usually get later. I feel that the casting director has been discussing it with the author or with the director and has a much clearer idea of what this character is than I do based on my reading of the script.

**SS:** We work with them but only as an adjunct to reading the script. But you can't get every single script read. Sometimes I get backed up because I also am reading books for some of my clients for future film projects. Some of my clients are now also directing. So there's a lot of reading to do. Clients like Brian Dennehy, Kathy Bates, and Greta Scacci, for instance, are involved with a lot of potential projects that I'm involved with. I try to be creative with the breakdowns. Certainly, I can't send a fifty-year-old for the role of a college student. But I send very few people for a part. If I send more than two, it's unusual. This is because I never represent any two actors who are that similar. Therefore no conflicts.

**What do you enjoy most/least about the work you do?**

**RB:** I swear and complain a lot, but I really love it. When I feel someone's right for a role and they get it, I'm thrilled. I mean a real role like a specific role in a book that is about to be written for the screen. I dream with my actors. The thing I don't like is that many of the people (casting directors) with whom we have to deal are not qualified for their jobs, which makes it very difficult. Many times then you're forced to go over their heads. That brings down somewhat of an insecurity when they find it out and then you have to repair that damage.

**MG:** Finding someone and helping them to become a star is very gratifying. It's upsetting when you lose a client that you've helped to develop. I believe it's mostly the younger kids coming up who don't understand the loyalty. They feel that by going with a larger agency they'll be packaged better. Let me tell you something, there are really only about six actors in America that you can really package. Another great part of this job is the acknowledgments. When Jane Anderson won the Emmy for the TV movie *The Confession of the Texas Cheerleader's Murder Mom* and said, "I want to thank my agent, Martin Gage," it was a great moment. When Debra Monk won the Tony and acknowledged the agency, that too was wonderful.

**HL:** The thing I enjoy most is finding new talent and helping it grow. The thing I enjoy least is losing that actor to a bigger agency.

**JW:** Most, I enjoy booking talent and discovering somebody. Least, it's a 120 million percent for 10 percent. That is, so much all consuming work for only 10 percent.

**MR:** What I enjoy most is saying, "You got the job." Also being there when one of my clients is honored for the work she's done. What I enjoy least is working with casting people who are not open to meeting people they've never met before, and are not open to meeting actors who've done one area of work and aren't being considered for another. What I mean is allowing that an actor who has done mostly theater can also do film. Or that an actor who's done mostly television can also do theater. Or dealing with the casting director that feels that an actor who's done only musicals can't do anything else but musicals.

**SS:** What I enjoy most is my clients. What I enjoy least is the whole business. It's not a very nice place anymore. I've had a company for almost twenty-eight years and I've watched the ethics, values, taste, and creativity slowly disappear.

### What is the one thing that actors do that really ticks you off?

**RB:** Call me and say, "What's going on?" Also when someone stops by and asks, "Do you have a minute?" Then twenty minutes later he's still there. I also dislike when actors ask for "feedback." If you know a casting director or a director very well and you do ask him on the actor's behalf, and then he tells you the actor was awful, what do you say then? I can't tell that actor that. What if he sees that casting director at a later time and says, "I heard you thought I was awful." I'll tell the actor they went taller, older, wider, whatever. Generally, the casting directors don't tell you.

**MG:** Lying. Not showing up for appointments. Sometimes an actor will say, "I don't want to play this part." Sometimes I know what actors can do better than they do. I try to help them by convincing them. Some actresses decide that they only want to play beautiful. Actors have visions of themselves that are restrictive. I've changed careers. I worked with Geraldine Page at a time when her movie career was pretty much over. She wasn't a leading lady anymore. I got her the Woody Allen movie *Interiors*. She didn't want to do it. I said, "What are you, crazy?" She said "That character's a fat, old matriarch." I convinced her to do it. God, how I loved that woman. She was a great, great actress. I sat at the Oscars with Rip Torn and her when she got the Oscar that night.

**HL:** Actors who don't have a sense of perspective. Not getting a costar on an episode is not the end of the world. I really get annoyed by actors who demand to speak to me, telling the receptionist it's urgent, only to find out that they only want feedback on an audition they had. Also I hate when actors are abusive to me, to a receptionist, to a casting director, or to a producer—when actors are nasty, screaming, or abusive.

**JW:** I think it's that many actors presume that it's all about them, their egos, the self-absorption. When I'll meet an actor socially and say, "Hi, how are you?" he'll tell me about his latest booking. Many actors don't look at agents as human beings but only as a way to get more work for themselves.

**MR:** When, at an audition, an actor is asked to make an adjustment and doesn't quite succeed. Then, when walking out the door he realizes what the director meant. Rather than turn around and ask if he can try it again, he just leaves. He has nothing to lose by asking. The worst he can hear is no. Something else that bothers me is the actor who shows up at an audition without a picture and résumé, assuming the agent already sent it in. Quite often the agent did, but the casting director hasn't opened that envelope yet. Another thing is showing up at an audition where they want you to sing and you bring only one song. They love it and ask you what else have you got? And you're left standing there. Another thing that gets to me is actors who don't take responsibility for their careers but put that responsibility on other people.

**SS:** An actor who calls every day and asks, "Am I up for anything?"

**What suggestions do you have for actors (a) to help themselves promote their work?; (b) to make themselves known to agents?**

**RB:** There's very little. Just keep on top of things, know what's going on. Network. Send pictures, tapes.

**MG:** Networking is very important. Do a showcase, do a play. Out here, some agents feel that booking an actor to do theater isn't profitable enough. There is a mentality out here, mostly among the younger agents at the bigger agencies, to only show big figures and go for only the big money. I tell my actors that they should do a play at least every two years. You can learn a lot of tricks in this business. Robert Pastorelli is one of my clients. He's about to star in a new series. He has leads in movies, does very well. Once every year or two, at the most, he does a show at the Ensemble Studio Theater or somewhere else. Just to keep at it. That's why he's so good. Never assume that you're there.

**HL:** Their job is to plant seeds and not expect to see results within any time frame. Find people that will champion you, that believe in you, and ask them to assist you in any way that they can. It's a business of who knows who. Talent always rises.

**JW:** Agents are not looking for actors that are looking for agents. Agents are looking for actors that are going places. If you're in a good showcase, someone will come to see it. Word travels, you'd be surprised. Every actor needs to find a "rabbi" within the office to champion him or her. The rabbi is that agent in the office that will promote him or her to other agents. Anyone who has ever succeeded in this business has had a champion.

**MR:** Get out there and get into something where your work can be seen. Create a vehicle for yourself like Chazz Palminteri or Eric Bogosian has done.

**SS:** As far as actors I don't represent—I don't particularly want or need to know what they're doing. I'm only really interested in the clients that I do represent. I'm not looking to broaden my talent base here. That's not to say if a twenty-two-year-old Robert Redford came to me I'd turn him away. As for the clients I do have, all I want for them to know is how to walk through the door and secure the job. It's called the art of auditioning. It's very different from being a wonderful actor. It can be taught and actors need to learn.

**What factors go into your choice of working with one actor over another?**

**RB:** It's hard to say. There's always something special. It's just the same as when you say on your door "By Appointment Only," and someone has the balls to come in and you look up. Next thing you tell the receptionist to let him in. I don't know what it is.

**MG:** As I said earlier, How can I sell this actor? What is so unique about him or her?

**HL:** It's a gut feeling and who I respond to the most. It's kind of like having a love affair. I've got to be passionate over his talent and potential. Negative people turn me off. Bad reputations travel fast.

**JW:** The actor's experience, what other people feel, what my gut feeling is, which actor I feel will make the most money. Who I feel will make the most money is probably the most important factor.

**MR:** Whether or not I think I can get him work, whether I feel I can work with him, whether I like him, whether I respect his talent.

**SS:** I must feel some passion for her talent. If I don't really believe in someone, how can I personally convince a casting director of her talent?

**If you had one piece of advice to offer actors regarding their careers or this business, what would it be?**

**RB:** If you want to act and you run into frustration in Hollywood or New York or Chicago, try to get with a theater company. Do something off or off-off or off-off-off! Also there are many other areas in the business. There are other types of jobs within the industry. But it's hard to tell someone that who just wants to act. There are production stage managers, executive producers, all kinds of creative work. Being an actor isn't everything.

**MG:** [laughing] Be a lawyer! Twenty years ago I would have said, Be a doctor! If you're young and are very dedicated, don't give up!

**HL:** Be nice to people. Don't look down on anyone. There isn't anyone in this business that isn't aching to move further up on the ladder just like you. Today's assistant is next week's agent. The guy that was in our mailroom nine months ago is now an assistant to one of the top agents at the Gersch Agency. To quote Marcia Schulman (casting director), "Figure out who you are and hold on for dear life."

**JW:** You have results or you have excuses. Anybody who's ever made it on any level has always been focused on the results.

**MR:** Study. If you were a musician, you'd be practicing every day. You want to get ahead—learn what you're doing.

**SS:** Probably, get out. You must really, really want it. Because the way that actors are treated is so revolting, you must have a tremendously tough skin to get through the process. This country does not have a tradition for respecting actors. There's only a tradition for idolizing movie stars.

**Is there anything else you'd like to suggest or comment on for a book of this nature?**

**RB:** Don't think you're going to make it on your looks. And don't get into this business because you want to make a lot of money. Be aware of what's going on. Be well rounded.

**MG:** This isn't the business I came into. It's changed tremendously. You can always tell the potential stars. The first star I ever worked with was Bernadette Peters, about twenty-five or thirty years ago. From the very first minute I knew. You couldn't stop Bernadette. There's no way she couldn't become a star. Same thing with Woody Harrelson. And this isn't just about talent. Talent isn't what gets you a job. Talent is what keeps you working. When Kim Basinger walked into my office for the first time—I knew. I thought, I can make this one a star in about eleven minutes. And I didn't know she could act. Her presence was unbelievable.

**HL:** Agents want you to succeed. Just as anywhere else in life, sometimes you will get screwed and sometimes you won't. But you can't walk around always expecting it.

**JW:** Actors must be prepared to be judged twenty-five hours a day. It's the hardest business in the world. You have to be able to tolerate an unhealthy amount of rejection and scrutiny. And quite often you're not even aware of who's judging you at what time. Embrace where you're making the money now and be satisfied. But always be looking for the next step. You're always auditioning.

**MR:** Instead of beating your head against the wall trying to get an agent to take responsibility for your career, create your own career. If your career's in a slump, you need to create a spin about yourself and I, as an agent, can't do it for you.

**SS:** I feel all actors should be trained. If you believe the assumption, and I do, that most directors aren't very good, you must be well trained so you can fall back on yourself. You must be self-reliant.

# Personal
# Managers

I contacted Gerard W. Purcell, national president of the Conference of Personal Managers (an organization of about three hundred
to four hundred personal managers) to discuss the role of personal
managers in an actor's career. Purcell has been the national president
of this organization for over twenty years. He has managed such
diverse talents as Maya Angelou and Al Hirt.

### What Managers Do

According to Purcell, "Most actors aren't born stars, their careers must
be developed. It's the manager's belief in the young actor that quite
often enables her to live up to her potential. Many managers put up
their own money to develop actors who they believe strongly in. They
act as mentors, coaches. Managers have a more personalized relationship with their clients. They are more instrumental in career
decision-making policy than agents are. They offer legal as well as
financial advice to their clients, introduce them to talent agents,
casting directors, publicists, anyone who can be of help in moving the
actor's career along. They arrange for auditions for their clients either

from the daily breakdowns, through agents, or with specific casting directors that they work with." Generally, managers work with only five to twenty-five clients. Personal managers are, according to Purcell, "in it for the big haul." They are not looking for the immediate commission. What they're interested in is, "What will be the impact if this artist succeeds?"

### Contracts and Commissions

Generally, managers request that an actor sign with them for three years with an option at the end of the third year for another two years. The reason for this more lengthy time period (than the standard agent's contract) is because of the amount of time it can take to develop and create interest in a (sometimes) unknown actor. Sometimes the manager will help the actor along by paying for better training for him or her, better wardrobe, or new headshots.

Because of the abundance of time and energy (and sometimes money) that they invest in their clients, they charge a slightly higher commission. The average commission is 15 percent. That's not saying that it can't be higher (it can be as much as 25 percent). It really has to do with the specific situation and particular actor and manager. It should also be mentioned that the percent that a manager receives is in addition to the 10 percent commission that the agent receives (if they worked together).

### Warning

Because managers are not franchised by the actors' unions, there are occasionally unscrupulous and unethical managers who take advantage of innocent talent. As with talent agents, it's always a good idea to ask to see the manager's client list. Also you should ask around and find out what type of reputation the manager has. Actors interested in more information on personal managers should contact the Conference of Personal Managers, 964 Second Avenue, New York, NY 10022. In California, contact Stanley Evans, Executive Director, Conference of Personal Managers, 10231 Riverside Drive, Toluca Lake, CA 91602.

# Interviews with Personal Managers

**M**ARILYN GLASSER (**MG**) of Basset Talent Management in New York City, spent eight years at Paramount Pictures. She was at ICM in business affairs for seven-and-a-half years, where she worked on contract negotiations. The last year and a half at ICM she was an agent. She presently handles about fifteen clients.

SID GOLD (**SG**) of Goldstar Talent Management has been in the business over thirteen years. Prior to that he worked in the New York school system.

SCOTT E. KREINDLER (**SK**) of Cyd LeVin and Associates decided to become a personal manager after working with a talent agency for a while and considering being an agent. This company has been in existence for seven years and handles a limited amount of clients.

---

**What does your job entail? What does a personal manager do?**

**MG:** A manager's primary function is to provide guidance and counseling to talent. That includes anything and everything, starting with the actor's presentation. I work mainly with new talent. If she's an up-and-comer, that means I help her learn what to do out there in the industry. How to look, how to walk, how to talk. It's teaching her that the minute you walk through the door, your audition begins (and knowing what that means). I took a girl who had been in this town for five years with nobody paying any attention to her. She had a lot of problems. She had personality problems, turned casting directors off. We had to address those problems. What I do is tell actors things they don't always want to hear, but sometimes it's necessary. Telling them things like their acting is not where it needs to be. If the bulk of the feedback I receive on their auditions indicates that they have talent but need to develop more, I tell them that point-blank. I believe in training anyway as an ongoing process. I know who the good acting coaches are in this town. I audit their classes if they permit me to. I am a great networker and I make it my business to find out who's out there teaching. I'm up-to-date on the best speech coaches, movement classes, improv classes, etc. It really has to do with what the client needs. I'm also available to help the client with wardrobe. Many actors don't know how they should look. So, as you can see, I deal with all aspects of the actor's career.

**SG:** We have an ongoing project of looking for and placing new talent in TV, film, theater, voice-overs, jingles, and print. We introduce actors to agents, casting directors, and producers. We also get them auditions. Our office will do a number of things to promote our talent. We have showcases with our clients in them. We invite casting directors, agents, producers. We do a lot of things in terms of promotion that agents can't or won't do.

**SK:** A personal manager and an agent do very similar things. On a very basic level, the agents get the actors their appointments. The manager helps the actors decide if they're going to go on the appointments. We are also involved with getting appointments for the actors and managing their careers. We help them to determine what's right for their careers, step-by-step. We have relationships with about twenty-four different agents. Anyone can hang a sign on his door and say he's a personal manager. Everyone here has either been an agent or has an agency background.

**Where do you find your clients? What do you look for?**

**MG:** It varies. Sometimes they're sent to me by agents, by other actors. I also find them at showcases, going to the leagues from the big schools, on Broadway, etc. I look for self-confidence. Someone who walks through a door and has an aura about them. Naturally, you look for talent and star quality.

**SG:** We go to a lot of showcases. We also go to theater camps like Stage Door Manor French Woods. We get a lot of recommendations for talent. Sometimes we advertise in *Backstage.* It really depends on what kind of project we're working on.
When we're looking for kids, we're looking for outgoing, fabulous personalities. With adults we look for a good look and some experience. With kids it's easier to get them started as long as they have the personality. With adults I find it a little harder.

**SK:** Anywhere. Everywhere. Agents will call me with clients who they feel need a manager. Let's say the actor just got a starring role on Broadway, the agent will call me to see if I might work with his client. There's two different kinds of clients that we will represent. We represent actors who have grown to the point where they need a manager. Perhaps the agent feels that if the actor doesn't get a manager he'll (the actor) move on to a bigger agent. We get the most satisfaction, however, out of developing actors' careers before they even have an agent. When you see star quality that just needs to be developed, it's very exciting.

**What should an actor look for when searching for a manager? What shouldn't he or she expect from the manager?**

**MG:** It's important that actors look for managers who have been in the business for some period of time and who understand the para-meters. You want a manager who "gets you." You want a manger who knows what's going on both in this town (New York City) and in Los Angeles, who has his finger on the pulse of the business. Actors should know what contracts are about. You should feel that the manager has the ability to sell you to casting directors, directors, agents, producers. The manager is a third eye for you. When you sign with a manager, you're no longer just with one individual who is in control of your career (the agent). It's really a team effort working for you.

**SG:** First of all, look for someone who's ethical, legitimate, and so on. Preferably the manager should be in the Conference of Personal Managers. Actors should look for someone who they feel they can get along with, someone they can trust, someone who they feel can really do something for them.

All managers do is get actors auditions. You'd be surprised how many actors seem to feel that it's our job to get them the jobs.

**SK:** A personal connection. Both the manager and the client should feel a passion for each other. Bottom line, the actor must feel a real trust in the manager. She must be willing to believe that this person is trustworthy and will be a strong guiding source for her career. There are actors who believe once they have a manager they don't have to do anything for their careers anymore. It'll just all be in the manager's hands. They give over the responsibility to the manager. That's just not the way it is. Actors must realize that it's a team effort. Actors must be out there looking for leads all the time. They can't wait for the agent or manager to do it for them.

### How do you decide which jobs are right for your clients?

**MG:** I don't decide, they ultimately do. To help them make the right choices, I make the actor aware of where he sits on the totem pole of things. Knowing where you are and in what point in your career will dictate the choices. You're always looking for growth and for movement. If you don't have videotape on yourself, you have to get some. You go from featured roles to supporting leads. From the supporting leads you have to go to leads.

**SG:** After interviewing clients, we try to find out specifically what talents they have. It really becomes about matching up the job requirements with the skills we feel that each of our clients has.

**SK:** It's always decided on a day-to-day basis. The breakdowns come out, we look at them, discuss them, and see what comes up. You try to be creative. As you get to know an actor, you sort of get a sense of what she wants and what she doesn't want. Again, it's a team effort. You must find out what type of roles and work get the actor passionate. Also, it's about shaping a career. You try not to limit an actor as to whether she's just a film actor or just a stage actor. You must go beyond that when casting. I have clients that in the same day will go up for a movie, a play, or a TV show.

**Can you describe the relationship managers have with talent agents? Casting directors?**

**MG:** Particularly in New York more than in Los Angeles, there has been a great resistance to managers. But I feel that's starting to change. The same could be said of casting directors. I've had a number of tremendous relationships with agents over the years and then I've dealt with agents that wouldn't give me the time of day. They just will not work with managers. The agents who are adverse to managers will say something like, "I want to have the relationship with my client." Or "I don't want you to take the client away from me." My feeling is, if it ain't broke, I'm not going to try to fix it. I generally work with bicoastal agents.

**SG:** We introduce our clients to specific agents. Different agents do different things. We presently work with about twelve different agents. Sometimes agents will call us and ask if we're handling anyone who is about eighteen to about twenty-five, such-and-such a type. We'll recommend someone to them. Basically, the same holds true with casting directors. But with most union projects, the casting director will call the union first. With nonunion work, we get a lot of calls directly from the casting directors.

**SK:** There are very few good managers in New York. Part of the problem is anyone can be a manager. Agents must be franchised (licensed) in New York. I'm with one of the good management agencies in the city.

Part of the problem between agents and managers is the insecurity that agents feel that managers are checking up on them. We don't work that way. We just try to do what we can to get the client in. We do our own submissions. Everyone in this office has relationships with the casting offices. So, instead of calling an agent and asking if he's submitted so-and-so for this project, we'll just submit her on our own. If the casting director okays the client for an audition, then we'll call the agent with the appointment information. As I've said, it's a team effort.

### What do you expect your clients to do to help promote their own careers?

**MG:** Network like crazy. They must do everything that they possibly can to help themselves. They must talk to other actors, find out who's in the know, the name of every theater company, and align themselves with the best of the best. They must keep up with already developed relationships, keep up their mailings. Actors must submit themselves for those nonpaying projects because you never know where the great opportunity is going to come from (even student films). At least meet the people on student films. You never know who they may become, the next Scorcese, Coppola.

**SG:** They must be readily available, well trained. We expect the actors to keep up their mailings, reminding people when they've booked work. Part of what they must always do is keep themselves fresh in their contacts' minds. Managers can't be expected to do that for them.

**SK:** First of all, they must be committed to doing good work, constantly staying fresh, taking classes, whatever. They must be prepared and ready for each audition that they get. They must have the confidence for each audition. Part of what we as managers do is instill the confidence in our clients that they need for the auditions.

**If you were to give actors any advice about their careers, what would it be?**

**MG:** Remember it's a business. Get your ego in check. Understand that you're the new kid on the block. You can do five independent films and everything might seem like you're going to take off and,... you can be yesterday's news tomorrow. Align yourself with a solid support system, not just flakes.

**SG:** I personally feel that every actor should have a manager. A good manager will get his clients work more than if they just have one particular agent. If a manager has faith in a client, he won't stop sending her out because she didn't book the last three auditions. Actors should realize that managers are in it for the long haul.

Another thing is it's not always the best idea to pick out your own headshot. Sometimes it's better to get a professional, subjective eye.

**SK:** I think that most actors have all of their own answers within their own grasp; all they must do is allow it in. Sometimes actors get really anxious and want some secret that will free them up. They must learn that it's within themselves.

# CHAPTER 21

# *Publicists*

**A** publicist is involved with many aspects of an actor's career, from molding an image to consulting on career decisions. Publicists arrange media interviews (television, print, radio), fashion layouts (if applicable), supervise photo sessions, create press materials, and give general advice—all of which help promote an actor's career. Campaigns vary depending on what the actor is doing. The bottom line is they attempt to make the person (or product) famous for whatever it is he or she does. They make up press kits that will include the actor's photo, bio, résumé, copies of any previous press they've had, etc.

### Do You Know Who I Am?

When the actor has a substantial role in a movie or play or has written a book that he or she wants publicized, the publicist will send out press releases to newspapers, magazines, television, and radio. Sometimes, however, the actor gets into legal or criminal trouble. At these times the publicist tries to keep the client out of the newspapers, or at the least give the criminal news a better "spin."

### Interviews with Publicists

MERLE FRIMARK (**MF**) heads her own public-relations company in New York City. The personalities she has worked with include Chita Rivera, Sir Ian McKellen, Sir Derek Jacobi, Angela Lansbury, Glenda Jackson, Peter O'Toole, Jessica Lange, André DeShields, Mark Hamill, Jessica Tandy, and Hume Cronyn.

CLAIRE O'CONNOR (**CO**) of the Claire O'Connor Agency has been a publicist for thirteen years. She has planned parties and garnered headlines for such clients as Mickey Rourke, Johnny Depp, Montel Williams, Governor Jerry Brown, and President Bill Clinton.

---

**At which point in his or her career should an actor contact a publicist?**

**MF:** An actor should contact a publicist when he has won a leading or featured role in a film, Broadway or Off-Broadway show, is on a television series, or finds himself with a unique cameo role that he feels will showcase his talent. It is certainly more difficult to publicize a chorus member or an actor with a very small role. When deciding to hire a publicist, an actor should not make this decision alone. He should consult with a manager or agent, and interview a minimum of four publicists.

**CO:** I think it's good to start early in a career, but the actor should have something going on. A young actor, not in a show, just starting out doesn't have much to promote.

**What should an actor expect from a publicist? What shouldn't he expect?**

**MF:** Again, much of this depends on what the actor is doing in which area of entertainment. It is important to always remember that there are no guarantees! Any publicist who says he will guarantee you certain coverage is not being honest, and the actor will probably be disappointed. If an actor can separate her performing persona from her business persona, she will be able to be more objective when planning her future.

**CO:** Actors can expect that publicists will get them press, get their names out there (within reason). If an actor is in an Off-Broadway show, let's say, but with a meaningful subject matter, or a trendy or timely subject, he can get better press. He shouldn't expect the cover of *Time* magazine unless he's mega big. But what he should and shouldn't expect really varies with the actor. One thing that shouldn't be expected, however, is any guarantee. It's all relative to what the actor is doing and what the writer is writing about this month or this year. If the actor has a good product, he can expect plenty of coverage.

### What determines the length of a relationship between a publicist and an actor?

**MF:** This varies greatly. If an actor is in a Broadway show, he may want to retain a publicist for the run of the contract. Many film actors and performers hire a publicist on an annual basis. Many publicists will only take a client for six months or more. Anything less than that is not realistic. A publicist needs enough time to test the waters, make contacts, and distribute press materials. National monthly magazines work three months in advance, and it does take time to generate media interest in any major city.

**CO:** It depends. If you're Bruce Willis you always have a publicist because you always have something going on. If you're constantly working or are a big star, you should always have a publicist. On the other hand, if you're going to do a show next month and you want people to know about you (and it), you may want to hire a publicist for that month, or hire her for a longer period to do follow-up. For example, you can be doing a show, hire a publicist, and she brings say fifty press people to see you. Ten of them may say, "In April, I'm going to be doing a story on young actors." It would be smart to make sure you've kept the publicist so she can get you in on that story. If you can afford it, it sometimes helps to have a publicist to do events like throw a birthday party for you and invite celebrities. Keeping your name out there even if you're not acting is also important.

### What are the financial considerations? How much should an actor be prepared to spend?

**MF:** It varies. Different agencies will charge varying fees. However, as in buying good clothing, we all know we get what we pay for. If a publicist charges an extremely low fee compared to others interviewed, chances are that actor should not expect high-end results. There are some high-profile stars who retain publicists to keep them *out* of the press. Regardless, the actor should keep within his or her own budget when hiring a publicist.

**CO:** From about $1,000 to $10,000 a month. It's difficult to say exactly what the actor gets per dollar. It has more to do with how much time and energy he expects from the publicist. Naturally, if the publicist is hired on a full-time basis, she will be making every effort to accomplish whatever it is that the client needs, publicitywise. Quite often, there are slow periods in actors' careers when there really isn't that much to promote. It's certainly a lot easier to get them in the columns when they have a hot movie or show about to open.

### Is there any advice you have for actors before they contact a publicist?

**MF:** Actors should be realistic and have an idea of what they hope to achieve from their relationships with a publicist. Oftentimes there is a relationship that can last for many, many years. They should be aware of their own limitations (e.g., preparing to do many interviews), and be prepared to open themselves up to the press.

**CO:** They should be prepared to carry through with it. They should have available time to do the interviews, photo shoots, etc. They have to really want it. You have to allow the publicist to do her job. Mainly, you must be available and willing to follow the advice you get. One problem I see all the time is the actor who doesn't want to do the small TV show interviews. He doesn't realize that quite often until he's done those shows it's hard to get him onto the bigger interviews. I have to get a tape of that small show and get it to the bigger ones to show that he's a good interview.

**When selecting a publicist, what should actors look for?**

**MF:** It is important that actors feel comfortable with and trust the publicist. This is a relationship based on trust and honesty. Actors should feel free to ask to see the publicist's client list.

**CO:** I think they should choose someone who has the time for them. A lot of big agencies who have a Bruce Willis or Robert Redford just won't have the time for you. The less-known actor cannot afford to not get what he wants for his money. Ask around for recommendations. Ask other actors, agents, and managers which publicist they've heard good things about. Then you should interview the prospective publicist. Don't just hire him on the phone after a short talk.

# *Promotional Gifts*

**P**romotional specialties come in all forms, from key rings with your name on them to pens, magnets, and mugs. They help to make potential agents, casting directors, and directors aware of who you are. They also keep your name in the minds of the people you've already met. As the Success Builders catalog says: "Give them a mug and they'll think of you with every cup of coffee. Give them pens and pads (with your name on it) so they'll think of you every time they jot down a phone number. It's the way to get your name noticed and remembered."

The Drawing Board Promotional Ideabook says: "Doesn't everyone you know carry keys? Make sure your name and service number are imprinted on their key chains. How many people do you know who haven't become completely dependent on Post-it® note pads? Get your imprint on the ones they have on their desk. Everyone uses a pen, right? An overwhelming 67 percent of businesspeople polled said they use some type of promotional product (according to the Specialty Advertising Association International)."

It should be mentioned that several of the casting directors and talent agents that I interviewed (see chapters 18 and 28) said that they found these "gimmicky gifts" annoying or offensive. It's up to you.

If this type of self-promotion interests you, you should request catalogs and more information from:

**Success Builders from Baldwin Cooke**
**2401 Waukegan Road**
**Deerfield, IL 60015-1588**
**800-231-2332**

The catalog includes the following self-promotional (your name on) items: hats, clocks, totes, pot holders, calculators, mugs, lights, road atlases, portfolios, drinkware, computer items, notepads, office accessories, giveaways, pens, key chains, magnets, buttons, and letter openers.

**Best Impressions Company**
**P.O. Box 802**
**La Salle, IL 61301**

The catalog includes writing equipment, leisure merchandise, office merchandise, giveaways, glassware, drinkware, key chains, tools, flashlights, executive gifts, clocks, and budget mugs.

**The Drawing Board Promotional Ideabook**
**P.O. Box 2995**
**Hartford, CT 06104**
**800-210-4431**

The catalog includes apparel, calculators, clocks, computer accessories, drinkware, giveaways, lights, notepads, portfolios, sports accessories, tools, totes, and travel and writing merchandise.

# *Producing Your Own Play*

**O**n occasion, a group of actors, or a single actor, finds a play that truly moves them and they decide to mount a full production. A project like this, to be done well, demands a great deal of time and energy. There must be the belief that the play can be fully realized with integrity and artistic truth. Just to do a production to "show your wares" quite often results in half-baked production values that look shoddy. The last thing you want is for your production to be labeled a vanity production. You and your company must be of the same mind and same vision.

### What Are Scene Showcases?

Rather than producing a full-length play, occasionally actors will get together and produce a "scene showcase night(s)" targeted at talent agents and casting directors. This is a team effort where all involved have agreed to put their time, energy, and money into a project created expressly to show off their talents.

The selected scenes may be related by a theme or totally arbitrary, depending on the needs and talents of the group. Generally, one of the actors in the group is selected to be the main producer, otherwise chaos may ensue.

Usually the group votes on all artistic and economic decisions concerning the event. A director and stage manager are hired or volunteered from within or outside the group.

### Things to Keep in Mind for a Scene Showcase

The group must decide on the following:

- A budget and how much they are willing to chip in for this event. Scene showcases can cost from several hundred dollars per person to over a thousand.
- A theater.
- How many nights the show will be performed.
- What kind of refreshments will be provided for the invited audience. This can be as simple as wine and cheese or much more extravagant.
- What jobs each member of the group will do. These volunteered chores include everything from mailings and phone blitzes of agents and casting directors, to painting scenery, buying and setting up the refreshments, and managing the stage and house.
- Casting.
- Selection of the order of the scenes.
- What kind of follow-up to agents and casting directors is needed after the event is over.

Both in New York City and Los Angeles there are a few professional groups that create these scene showcase evenings. Their fees vary as do the quality of the evenings. Before signing on with one of them, ask if you can attend one of their showcase evenings.

### Producing

To produce a play in a showcase situation can be very complex and demanding. If it's a new play, there can be many months of rewrites and development before a production should be mounted. If your group is optioning a play (paying royalties), there should be a few readings to see if the play works well for the actors. In both instances, you might want to think about a fund-raising benefit to help with the costs of producing.

Again, I think it's important to mention that this kind of venture should stem primarily from a love of the play, not as a means of promoting yourselves as actors. That being said, here are some things to think about before taking on such a large task.

### Skills Needed to Produce

- *To produce a play you must have good organizational skills.* You will be arranging everything from casting to hiring a director to raising the money for the production to finding a theater. You must be a person who can deal with detail and minutiae. The producer is at the top of the totem pole. It's your vision that can either make or break the production.
- *You'll need excellent business skills.* It'll be your responsibility to raise the money for your production and to handle all the expenses. Part of having good business skills is being able to negotiate with people, keeping accurate financial records, etc. The average Actors Equity showcase costs between $8,000 and $10,000. It's advisable never to use your own money, unless you can afford to take on such an expense. In some cases, the members of the cast either all chip in or do some type of fund-raising event to get the money for the production.
- *You must have promotional skills.* Unless you have the ability to get people to come see your show, it'll be a somewhat wasted effort. Getting newspaper critics, for instance, can be very difficult. You'll want to get agents and casting directors to come see your work—also not an easy task. Even getting a good audience night after night can be quite a chore. You must start your mailing and phone campaigns way in advance of opening night. The whole thing is a matter of persistence, diplomacy, and tact.

### Exactly What Does the Producer Do?

- Oversees the budget for the show
- Hires or finds a director
- Finds the theater

- Arranges for the casting of the show
- Hires or finds a scenic designer
- Hires or finds a lighting designer
- Hires or finds a stage manager
- Is responsible for all legal obligations
- Hires a publicist if financially possible
- Finds the best insurance for the production
- Hires a ticket agency if it fits into the budget
- Is responsible for having tickets and programs printed up
- Finds rehearsal space for the actors
- Has to deal with any problems with the cast, the director, the scenic designer, and the landlord

### The Reading

Don't even think of producing a show unless you've had at least one reading (preferably a few) of the play. In the case of a new play, what looks good on paper doesn't always make for a good evening of theater. Some plays read well but don't play well, and vice versa. Even if the play you've chosen is well known and has been produced many times, the reading is a great opportunity for you and your fellow actors to experience the roles you'll be playing and to see how an audience responds to the play. Since there will be an invited audience, you'll also be able to get some sense of the production's potential. Use a tape recorder to tape the reading. It's not advisable to invite casting directors and agents to these preliminary readings. The whole purpose of the reading is to try out the play, not audition for casting directors. With, at best, a few rehearsals, you shouldn't expect too much from the reading. If the reading(s) goes well and the response has been positive, then perhaps you might consider going to the next step on the ladder—a fully realized production.

### Preproduction

There are certain times of the year when it is not advisable to open a showcase. The Christmas holiday season (mid-December) through the first week in January is a difficult time to get people in to see your show, as is most of August. If you're planning a summer production in the city (when theater rentals are less expensive), you'll find that your audiences will be thinner, especially on weekends since many people go away. And you'd better be certain that the theater you've chosen has a reliable air-conditioning unit or you'll see many people in the audience flee at the first intermission—or sooner!

It's very important that there is constant communication during the preproduction period between the members of the company (as to how things are moving along). Try to keep everyone posted as to significant production details as they are arranged. Things like the production dates and the theater must be announced as they are decided so that everyone is kept abreast of what is happening.

### Looking at Theaters

One way to begin finding that right theater for your production is by asking around and gauging the theater's reputation. Generally, certain theaters have a buzz on them, both good and bad. If they've been unkind or unfair to actors in past productions, it'll get around. You should also make it your business to start going to showcases around the city to see the different theaters.

### Criteria for a Good Theater

- Check out the location of the theater. Is it near public transportation? In a pleasant neighborhood?
- What condition is the theater in?
- How are the acoustics? Size of the stage, etc.?
- Is it well ventilated? Too cold? Too warm?
- Is the house staff polite? Organized?
- Are there clearly marked fire exits?
- Is there an area to store furniture? Props?
- What is the backstage area like? Is it safe? Sanitary?

### Before Signing the Contract for the Theater

- Remember, no Equity showcase can be performed in a theater having more than ninety-nine seats.
- Never sign a contract for the theater until you've had at least

one meeting with the theater manager to iron out all details.

- Most theater rental prices are negotiable (if not for money, then for services).
- Be clear on all of the terms of the rental agreement. There should be no gray areas. It is always to your advantage to have a lawyer look at the contract.
- Some pertinent questions you should ask:
  - Is all the equipment in the theater included in the rental, or do I have to bring in anything of my own for a production?
  - Will the actors be given rehearsal time in the space during the day?
  - Does the theater handle phone reservations and have a ticket booth?
  - Are deposits refundable?

### Allotment of Money for a Showcase

You will need to budget all expenses for your production in advance. Here are some of the major costs that producers must keep in mind when producing an Equity showcase:

- The rental of the space (the theater). Theaters on theater row in New York City can cost up to $2,000 per week. Theaters Off-off Broadway and L.A. waiver theaters can run $100–$200 per night. The more out of the way the theater is, the less it will probably cost.
- Rehearsal space. Sometimes rehearsal space is included with your theater rental. Generally, rehearsal space starts at $12 per hour and can be as high as $25 per hour and more.
- Insurance for your production. Mandatory by Equity and in most theaters. The amount varies depending on your specific situation and the theater.
- Fliers and mailing expenses. This is your main means of advertising. Fliers should be as elaborate as you can afford. It is, after all, the first impression your potential audience member gets about your production. This can cost your company as little as a few hundred dollars up to thousands of dollars, depending on your budget.

- Costume costs. Sometimes your cast can bring their own costumes. When you do period plays, costume rentals can soar.
- The set for your production. Many companies build their own sets. Once you hire professionals to build and paint your scenery, you're running into a big expense, especially if there are multiple sets.
- Prop costs. Quite often your cast can bring their own props.
- A ticket agent. It's not always necessary.

### A Union or Nonunion Show

Somewhere early in the planning of your production you will have to make a very important decision: union or nonunion. If you yourself are a member of Actors Equity and wish to star in this play, there really isn't much choice. Equity actors may only perform in Equity-approved showcases! Don't try to play around with this rule; it's not worth it. Actors who aren't members of Actors Equity, however, may perform in Equity showcases. If you are nonunion and decide to produce a nonunion showcase, you're pretty much on your own. Even if you choose to go nonunion with your show, you still must deal with state health laws, personal/work ethics, public safety, and many other producer headaches. The main advantage you have in a nonunion show is that you don't have the union breathing down your back with any rules or regulations of how your show must be produced. Also, there is a lot less paperwork.

If, however, you opt for a union show, you have to contact the business representative in charge of Equity showcase productions at Actors Equity. In New York City, the address is 165 West Forty-sixth Street, New York, NY 10036. The telephone number is (212) 869-8530. You must apply for your Equity showcase application fourteen days before you begin casting or start rehearsals, whichever comes first.

### The Equity Showcase Code

Actors Equity defines an Equity showcase as "a not-for-profit production in which AEA members elect to participate for the purpose of presenting plays and/or scenes in limited performances for the benefit of participating members."

- The show can only be performed in New York City. (The waiver theater in L.A. has similar rules. Check with Equity for theaters outside of New York City.)
- It must receive the express consent of Actors Equity.
- The show can be produced only by individuals, groups of individuals, and/or not-for-profit institutional theaters that have not been prohibited from doing so by contract or prior agreement. Any producer on the Equity list of defaulting producers shall be not be accorded the privileges of the Showcase Code.
- Your total budget must be under $15,000 ("the one-shot producer").
- You can only have up to twelve performances within four weeks (but can get four additional performances if needed).
- You can charge only up to $12.
- Complimentary tickets must be made available to industry people.
- Equity must receive the following information from you prior to your initial casting:
  - The dates of all rehearsals and performances.
  - The cast list (available roles).
  - Either your address or the address of someone you designate where Equity actors can send their photos and résumés for consideration for roles in your production.
- Also keep the following in mind:
  - You must reimburse the cast and crew for transportation costs for all rehearsals and performances that they attend.
  - All Equity members must be comped in (free) to see your show if there are available seats at that performance.
  - Actors in your production are entitled to have their photos displayed in the lobby and a copy of their bios printed in the play program.

### The Actors Equity Code Regarding Publicity/Advertising

All advertisements, other than paid newspaper ads or broadcast advertisements, but including fliers, posters, brochures, invitations, etc. must include the following:

- The names of all AEA members involved in the production with an asterisk (*) before their names.
- Paid newspaper and broadcast advertisements must use the phrase "Equity-Approved Showcase." In addition, if the names of the theater, play, and author are used in the advertisement, then the names of all AEA members must be included.
- Programs must be given free to all audience members.
- All programs must include a "Who's Who" (with the AEA member having final approval of all biographical material).
- Eight-by-tens of all AEA members must be displayed prominently in the front of the house.

# The One-Person Show

**P**erhaps one of the greatest showcases an actor can have is the one-person play. It is just you alone on the stage in front of the audience. But if your only reason for doing a one-person play is just to be seen, please let me advise you here and now, don't. What I've discovered in the interviews that follow is that the only reasons for putting yourself through this extremely difficult and time-consuming process should be the love of the play, the character, and/or the character's beliefs and ideals. If your motivation is purely self-promotional, to be seen, more likely than not you will fail. And a failed performance will be judged as nothing more than a vanity production. The scrutiny to which you are subjected in a one-person play is much harsher than being in the cast of a regular play. Fore-warned is forewarned.

If, however, you have found or written a one-person play that passionately excites you, then certainly you should go for it. Finding producers for your one-person play may be difficult so you may have to produce it yourself, which is not usually a good idea. If the play has previously been produced, you may have to pay royalties for each performance. If it's a new work, there may be a period of development and rewrites with the playwright attending rehearsals. If you've written the play yourself, you'll need a third eye to help you shape the piece, as well as perform in it.

The director you choose to work with on this play must be someone whose opinion you trust implicitly. Because of the nature of a one-person play, you should be prepared for an intimate, intense collaboration with your director. The director's vision must be similar to yours.

And, finally, you must be prepared to work for a long time on the play, perhaps years. One way to gauge your progress is to have readings and performances of the piece before an invited guest audience.

As you can see, it's a tremendous amount of work requiring a total commitment. But if you're determined and your dedication to the play is total, and you have the talent to pull it off, it can be the greatest theatrical experience of your life.

### Interviews with Actors in One-Person Plays

ROB BECKER (**RB**) began doing stand-up comedy in 1981. In 1989 he appeared on *Late Night with David Letterman*. In 1988 he began working on his one-man show, *Defending the Caveman*. It has had sold-out runs in San Francisco, Dallas, Philadelphia, Washington, D.C., Chicago, and New York City. It had sold out performances at the Helen Hayes Theatre since March 1995 and was the longest running one-person play on Broadway.

JOAN RATER (**JR**) has performed her one-woman show, *Make the Brothers Stop*, at the New Jersey Shakespeare Festival (The Downtown, Out of Town series), Dobama Theater in Cleveland, West Bank Cafe, HERE, Greenwich Street Theater, and the Group Theater in Seattle. The piece was a finalist at the Actors Theater of Louisville's Flying Solo Festival. She most recently performed the piece in Denmark.

PAUL ZALOOM (**PZ**) won an Obie for his performance-art piece *The House of Horrors*. The piece originated at the Dance Theater Workshop and was later performed at the American Repertory Theater in Cambridge. His solo shows were also performed at Theater for the New City, the Performing Garage, the Manhattan Punchline, and the Vineyard Theater. His nine solo shows received eight European tours and numerous national tours. He is presently performing on the CBS show *Beekman's World,* an educational science show for kids (although adults make up 55 percent of the audience).

COLIN MARTIN's (**CM**) show *Virgins and Other Myths* was called "riveting," "emotionally charged," and "remarkably candid" by the *New York Times.* He performed the show at Primary Stages in New York City and then it moved off Broadway for a very successful run. Prior to New York City, the piece was performed in several theaters in Los Angeles in 1994–95. Most recently, he appeared as Prior in *Angels in America* at ACT in San Francisco. Other credits include Charles Ludlam's *Camille* at the Highway Theater in L.A. and guest-starring roles on *ER,* and in the films *Crimes and Misdemeanors, Three of Hearts,* and *Majorettes.* He is a member of Artists Confronting AIDS.

---

**First, a little information about your piece. What's it about? Its genesis?**

**RB:** Basically, it's about the gender gap. It's about men and women, their differences, the gap in communication between them. I use my wife and my marriage as an example.

**JR:** It's generally about one woman's search for self-esteem. That woman is essentially me, although there are fictitious parts to the show, too. It's basically me telling stories of my struggle and search for self-esteem. I had just moved back to New York from the Milwaukee Rep. and wasn't getting much work as an actress. I was looking for a way to get myself some work. Tony Phelan, my husband, suggested that I start writing down the stories of what was going on with me. It started as just a way to deal with my feelings—journal writing.

**PZ:** *The House of Horrors* piece consisted of three sections, "The House of Horrors," "Safety Begins Here," and "Yikes!" "The House of Horrors" is a piece about indoor pollution. I was really interested in the idea that the average American home has about four thousand chemicals in it. After we build our houses we make them airtight to conserve energy and so we live in this chemical stew. Most of these chemicals are known to be carcinogenic. The piece is a puppet show using dummy or doll puppets about eighteen inches tall. It's about how the house, the carpeting, the couch, and the wallboard all collectively kill the family. It's a slapstick, wild comedy.

**CM:** It's about sexuality, power, and innocence at different points in a person's life; how sexuality evolves and changes. I use the theme of virginity, which is a universal concept or condition as a starting-off point to explore sexuality. I tell my own story, my experiences, my personal journey to explore these themes.

**How did you get it started? How long before your first production? Were you pleased with that production? What did you learn?**

**RB:** I started writing *Defending the Caveman* in 1987. I was doing stand-up comedy and I started including pieces of it in my stand-up routine. In 1991, I put it up at the Improv in San Francisco. It took three years from the time I started writing it until the first public production. I was pleased with the response. It ran for four months. One thing I realized is that it's far different to have something on paper than it is to do it onstage. What looks good on paper sometimes feels a little stiff or uncomfortable onstage. I really had to kind of tailor it to myself. I'd talk to people after the show, get feedback. I had some pieces in there that were really funny and got huge laughs, but then I realized from the feedback that it made the wrong point. In a one-person show like this where there's a theme, a story, a beginning, middle, and end, where you're trying to make points along the way, you have to give up stuff if it makes the wrong point.

**JR:** Right around that same time my friend Amy Rosenfield was starting a theater company called the Working Playground. We'd meet once a week and present work we were working on. I presented some of these writings as a solo piece—short segments of ten minutes or so. I started gaining confidence in the piece and at the same time learned what worked and didn't work. It took me about two years until the first presentation [at the Greenwich House Theater]. I had about twenty solid minutes of material and about an hour of somewhat connected material with a deadline to meet. Around August I took a leave of absence from my job and went to Cleveland with my director [husband], Tony Phelan, and we did nothing but work on the piece for three solid weeks. I was having trouble writing the material down so I worked with a tape recorder and he'd later transcribe it. What came out on the tape is what we kept in the show; we hardly changed a word. Next, we shaped the piece, cutting away unnecessary material, and then we rehearsed it. The first performance—a dress rehearsal for friends and a publicist—was awful! I was nervous and felt it was bad. The next night, however, was incredible! People laughed and were moved. One thing I've learned is that you have to keep your show technically simple. Quite often at festivals you're not given much time to tech your show.

**PZ:** I had played at Dance Theater Workshop with my previous program. Dance Theater Workshop is a very good, very visible venue for alternative performance and dance. I asked David White, the producer, if he'd produce my new show and he said yes. Generally, my shows had a two-year cycle. I did a new show about every two years. A show would be created while I was touring with another show. Money was raised through grants and earned income to finance the new show.

As far as being pleased with the show? Yeah, it went the way I wanted it to go. And no, I didn't get the response I wanted. I wanted a hit, a long-running, Off-Broadway show. And that was not the response I got. My idea was to do the off-off thing and get a producer with some money to move it. The joke is I'm like a television star now and people think that that's the apex of my career, my goal. But to be an independent artist, to create things out of your head, that is on your own agenda, and that makes you nuts—to do that is far more fulfilling. Doing the solo shows was much more rewarding than doing TV.

**CM:** I was in Los Angeles working with a group called Artists Confronting AIDS. The work was going great but I was broke, thinking I might have to leave L.A., go back home to Madison, Wisconsin, and get a nine-to-five job. I just wasn't interested in becoming a generally successful actor on TV. But I thought, before I leave L.A. the one thing I have to do is write something. I hadn't written anything since I was a teenager. Simultaneously, I had read a book called *A Rock and a Hard*

*Place* by Anthony Godby Johnson, a teenager, who was infected with AIDS by a friend of the family who had sexually abused him. I was very moved by it. I'm basically a very private person, reticent. But it just seemed like this was the right time. That was the genesis.

**What obstacles have you encountered in performing in your own show? In producing your own show (if you did)? How did you eventually overcome them (if you did)?**

**RB:** It's extremely difficult to get anybody to put on your show when you're new. Finding theater space is difficult. That's why I started in a comedy club. I did produce this show at one point. The problem I had in producing was that the Improv wasn't putting much into advertising, so I had to put some in. Luckily this show has always succeeded on word of mouth. Because of the show's reputation (from San Francisco), the Improv asked me to do it even though it wasn't finished. The first few weeks were rough. I was rewriting all day long, putting it on stage at night, and then going home to do more rewrites. I didn't have a third act. I'd do the first and second act, and then at the end I'd come out and tell the audience, "Here's what I'm working on." And basically I'd tell them my ideas for that third act. It was weird but it worked. Even when it was that rough, people were out telling their friends about the show.

**JR:** The biggest lesson I learned is that I needed to get a really good videotape. I went through about four different tapes before I found the right tape. A lot of it is close-ups and it cuts back and forth. It was taped live before an audience, which I recommend everyone do. And you've got to edit it. Tape it about three times and select the best from each tape. Sending the tape out is an important part of your marketing. I've sent the tape out about fifty times. You hardly ever get a copy back. The tape is fifty minutes long. Most of the festivals want the tapes to be under an hour. My feeling is that most people watch only about five minutes of your tape, so I suggest that you cue it up to a really strong section of your piece. I've produced productions of this piece at The West Bank Cafe and at HERE. The most difficult aspect of producing was getting an audience—the constantly being on the phone, sending out cards, and begging people to come. Publicity is definitely the hardest thing.

**PZ:** My work was not readily adaptable to the Off-Broadway audience. It tended to be more political and somewhat didactic. I was hoping to be relentlessly entertaining but maybe I was just too low rent, too eccentric, too out there for Off-Broadway. I was paid by the venue—a fee. There were also the grants. At Dance Theater Workshop they provide the services there to independent artists, unlike any other venue in America. They are the most service-oriented, arts service organization in the world for performance artists. They give you a kit that tells you how to produce yourself in New York and guidance on how to build a career.

**CM:** I mentioned to a friend of mine in mid-December of '93 that I wanted to do this and she said, "Great, let's produce it!" Realizing she was serious about producing, I wrote the piece in about two weeks. I set up two workshop dates, January 9 and 16 of '94 at Noho Studios in North Hollywood. I had been producing a theater series there for Artists Confronting AIDS. Ten days before I opened I got a director, Bruce Blair. The whole thing was a big adrenaline rush. See, I hadn't written any of it down, it was all in my head. A lot of people came to see it and were very encouraging. We got a booking from that production at Highways Theater (Tim Miller's space). And then a work-in-progress at the Zephyr Theater in March. I was afraid that my story would only be of interest to me. I learned that there was interest in my story; other people found it compelling. I realized I had to do work on the dramatic structure and theatrical integrity of the piece. I didn't want to do just vignettes. I wanted to create a journey, a play with a beginning, middle, and end. I realized I had to be patient, that I had a lot of work ahead of me.

The main obstacle that I found was that some theaters felt that any play that deals with gay sexuality is a "gay play." And if one gay play is done a year, that's the quota. People want to pigeonhole plays.

At the beginning, I produced the play myself. Bruce Blair and I were very grassroots. We did a lot of the fund-raising as well as co-producing it with Geo Hartley in Hollywood. I walked the streets and put up fliers, whatever. Everyone should do that. That's what it takes.

**How did you go about finding the creative team for your show?**

**RB:** I directed it myself. I had an acting coach come in for the first couple of weeks to give me some notes. So, in a sense, I was my own creative team.

**JR:** My director basically did all that. In the original production, Amy Rosenfield (the producer) did that stuff.

**PZ:** Dance Theater Workshop provides a lighting designer. I hired a consultant, Gordon Edelstein, during the rehearsal period. He had worked with me at the Berkshire Theater Festival. We worked together to polish the piece. It was the first time I had somebody from the outside help out. I later went on to have other directors work on my pieces.

**CM:** Originally, my friend Mindy Kanaskie produced it. She brought in Bruce (the director) and my collaboration with him has been invaluable.

**What have you learned from this experience? What achievement regarding this project are you most proud of?**

**RB:** Theaters sometimes are very strange when it comes to business. There seems to be some noble thing about losing money. You can go into these theaters and say, "I have this huge hit, this one-person show." And you get all this resistance because you're not Mamet or someone. The main thing I've learned is you just have to believe in yourself and what you're doing.

**JR:** Just that I have been able to affect people on an emotional level. That's what I like to see in theater. And I feel this piece takes an audience on an emotional journey. I'm a better actor because of my work on this piece. My timing is much better. The thing I keep thinking backstage every time before I do my show, my objective, is to try to make the audience understand me. Originally the show was much more intense, much more dramatic. Now it's much funnier. I think the show is easier to watch. If I sense people are uncomfortable, I won't look at them anymore, because I know they want me to leave them alone.

**PZ:** My interest has always been to get people to laugh about things that are essentially going to kill them. Lord Buckley (a beat comedian of the fifties) and Peter Schuman of the Bread and Puppet Theater were my two biggest inspirations. Buckley said—I'm paraphrasing— "It is the duty of the humor of any given nation in time of crisis to attack that crisis in such a way as to get the audience to laugh so they don't die before they get killed."

**CM:** As an actor, it's the toughest role I've ever done. It's very hard to get up there, be honest, and just connect with yourself. I've learned that when I honor who I am rather than try to change or alter who I am, my life and work take on an amazing energy and the results are incredible. It's very empowering. If you don't shout out into the world, you can't get a response back since you don't give the world anything to respond to. The payoff is the letters and phone calls I get from people. When audience members stay after the show and tell me how they've identified, how they've connected, it's very rewarding.

### What advice do you have for other actors considering this type of project?

**RB:** You have to really believe in your piece. If you really do, other people will too. You have to be willing to put your own money into it in the beginning. Keep mailing lists. I have a mailing list of fifty thousand. I let my audience know what's going on, if I've been extended, where I'm going next, like that. That's how I got such a big advance sale here in New York. It was the biggest advance the Helen Hayes Theatre has ever had. The way it looks now, I'll be breaking the records for one-person shows on Broadway. Jackie Mason's show ran 367 performances; Lily Tomlin's ran 398. I should be passing them this August. I'm a big believer in setting goals. Broadway was a goal I set for myself. [Becker did break the record.]

**JR:** In my opinion, the most affecting solo shows are in-your-face, raw, and personal. Be direct with the audience. Tell us something we haven't heard before. Keep it to under an hour. Be aware of pacing—keep it moving. Be aware of how your audience is. Workshop your piece for six months to a year with a group of people you trust.

**PZ:** It's really great being an artist and doing your own art and not having to rely on someone else to write for you. I came from a community (performance artists) where relentless self-promotion was not looked on kindly. I don't advise creating a performance piece to launch yourself into Hollywood. It must be compelling; something that you are doing for yourself. But for an artist to be successful, you must find ways to promote yourself. I was relentless about promoting myself. My approach was to take a lot of photographs. I hired a photographer, did a twelve-to-fourteen-hour photo session where four hundred to six hundred pictures were taken. And then I had about twenty-five original and about six bulk prints made up. So there were hundreds of prints offered as exclusives to major papers, and the bulk ones sent out. Dollar for dollar it was the best investment possible. The whole thing was a couple of grand, but I got hundreds of thousands of dollars worth of free publicity.

**CM:** This piece is not about trying to get affirmation or validation of my experiences. It's not about therapy or portraying myself as a victim. I wanted to create a piece of theater that had integrity as a piece of theater. If other actors want to draw from what I'm saying about myself, they're welcome to. But basically I don't like to give advice.

# Independent Films

**T**here are a great many opportunities for actors working in independent films. Aside from acting in them, many actors are now also producing, directing, and/or writing their own movies. For the same price it would cost to produce an Off-Broadway show, you can now make your own independent film. Many actors have started taking filmmaking and screenwriting classes in hopes of eventually producing, and starring in, their own films.

Chazz Palminteri wrote and performed his one-man show, *A Bronx Tale*, with the specific intention of having it made into a film with him starring in it. Robert De Niro saw Palminteri's show and, indeed, did produce the movie version with him in it. Many actors are taking Palminteri's lead and are writing their own one-person shows, hoping for the same results.

One thing I've discovered in researching this topic is that there are a great many ways to go about making an independent film. Each filmmaker I met with seemed to have gone about it her own way. I felt that to truly give this topic (filmmaking) a fair discussion would take much more than just one chapter in a book such as this. What I think might be more helpful is to refer you to some excellent books on the subject. Also, please check out the actor/filmmaker interviews at the end of this chapter.

### Helpful Books

If you feel that you have the potential to be a screenwriter, I'd like to recommend the following books: *Four Screenplays* (Dell) by Syd Field, *Writing Great Screenplays for Film and TV* (Arco) by Dona Cooper, and *Writing Scripts Hollywood Will Love* (Allworth) by Katherine Atwell Herbert.

For actors with an interest in directing and/or producing films, I suggest the following books: *Making Movies* (Dell) by John Russo, *All You Need to Know about the Movie and TV Business* (Fireside) by Gail Resnick and Scott Trost, and *Feature Filmmaking at Used-Car Prices* (Penguin) by Rick Schmidt.

### Why Experienced Stage Actors Are a Plus for Independents

I had an enlightening discussion with Robert Hawks, a professional independent film consultant. His company, Independent Consulting for Independents, assists film directors and writers by critiquing their scripts and then looking at the rough cuts to assess what potential they may have in the marketplace. Hawks also helps filmmakers select which festivals the film might be right for and helps select potential distributors to be targeted for a particular film. He has been on the advisory committee at the Sundance Film Festival (as well as many other festivals) and is also a film curator and programmer.

He explained how significant a good role in a well-received independent film could be in bringing an actor's talents to the public's eye. He pointed out that "actors can find meatier and far more substantial roles in the independents," and went on to say that, "Having a strong theater background can be very helpful when working on independent films." Because of the economics involved, these films have to be shot quickly. Often there will only be a couple of takes. The actor must be well prepared. Good theater training is vital. "Some independents have the luxury of a rehearsal period prior to the film's shooting. An actor who's well trained in theater can utilize the rehearsal period to deepen his work on the character and focus his performance. Stage actors know how to rehearse, how to concentrate, and how to repeat the same thing over and over without getting stale. They are more disciplined in their craft. Naturally they are a real plus on an independent film set."

### Ways to Find Work in the Independents

Agents receive daily breakdowns on many of the independent films that are casting. The trade papers constantly list auditions for them. On occasion, some independent films receive readings at different theaters on off nights (Monday or Tuesday). Check the trade papers to see when they are scheduled.

### Interviews with Actor/Filmmakers

PATRICK INZETTA's (**PI**) film *Grace Has Mace* was a short (half-hour), black-and-white film. He coproduced, cowrote and codirected this film with Juli Berg. The film has been entered in several national and international film festivals.

MICHAEL NEELEY's (**MN**) *Badges* is a forty-five-minute color TV pilot.

---

### How did you get the idea to make your own independent film?

**PI:** Juli [his partner] had made several short films, and I had acted in several short films. We use to talk about ideas for films and then one day Juli said, "Why don't we make one?" So we sat down and started work on the script. This was my first screenplay. It took us a good year to get the script finished.

**MN:** A couple of years ago, a friend of mine and I were driving into the city and were discussing the differences between us. He was Italian, born in Italy, raised in New York, and I was from the Midwest. We started imagining what it would be like if we were teamed up as cops. Then, about eight months ago I was approached by a director I knew who said he wanted to put together some video shorts for his director's reel. At around that same time an attorney friend of mine, who had worked on putting together a cable access program that had fallen through, mentioned that he was looking for a project to replace it. So everything kind of fell into place. My friend and I decided that we'd write up the script. The director would get his short for his reel, and my lawyer friend would get a replacement for the project that he'd done all this groundwork on.

### What did you need to know before beginning?

**PI:** We started breaking down how we visualized it, using storyboards. We storyboarded all of our camera shots. Also we scouted locations in New York. Juli and I were going to codirect, and I was also going to act in it. Our actors were actors that I knew from around. The salaries were deferred since there really wasn't any money budgeted to pay actors. With things like sound, however, we had to put money up front to pay a sound technician. Sound is important and not something you can skimp on. The film wasn't made as a commercial venture; it was made to show people what we could do, our potential.

**MN:** I was the actor, writer, and producer on the project—a lot of hats. We started having meetings to develop and write a script. We formed a limited liability company. The script took about a month to finish. Next we did a staged reading. We cast actors, rented a theater space, invited an audience, and even had questionnaires for the audience to fill out about the reading. After the reading, we had a question and answer period; then, we made some adjustments in the script and set up a time to do the shooting.

### How did you begin? Where do you start?

**PI:** We owned our own cameras, which saved us the rental fees for cameras. We shot on 8 mm. Everything was planned in advance. What we were doing was guerrilla filmmaking. For instance, we didn't have permits or things like that. Juli had worked in an editing facility and later on we bartered time for editing. You must understand everything was on a shoestring. We did make up a budget. The price of the film was expensive, as was developing. We edited the film by transferring it to video [and then doing the editing on a computer].

Sound is a big expense. Props, costume, food, these are all things that we budgeted. The film cost $7,000. It took us three years from start to finish [including editing, postproduction, etc.]. The reason it took so long was because of everyone's schedule. We met maybe once or twice a month. It was a very loose shooting schedule—weekends, mornings, late at night, whenever we could. The actual shoot took place over one year, probably around forty shooting days.

**MN:** First, of course, there's the budget. You have to figure out what things will cost. You go through each department on the film and see what your needs will be. We wanted to shoot our film on 35 mm, but changed that to a high-grade beta that transfers easily to film. The other major expenses on our film were craft services [meals], editing, and sound. We did the film as a nonunion shoot. We sent full breakdowns to every agent and manager in town. We got a great response to the breakdowns. The casting call took place in three stages: the general audition, the callbacks, and then a screen test. I strongly advise you to screen-test for a movie if you can. We put together the crew at the same time. We got a line producer who scouted locations, got our insurance, permits, etc. Just so you know, the insurance policy is usually $1 million for these shoots and costs about $5,000 (depending on what and how you're shooting). We got our permits through an NYU [New York University] affiliation. If you want to get a permit to shoot, it's not that difficult. You just have to show them proof of insurance and tell them where you want to shoot [your shooting schedule]. The shoot took two weeks [six days a week].

**Any advice on the day-to-day shooting?**

**PI:** I learned that it's very difficult to direct a film that you're acting in, especially the first time out. It's definitely something I don't recommend to other actors if they don't have to.

We did about three takes for each shot. We had to be sure we had it because we were shooting in black and white and had different film exposures.

For us, the most expensive thing in the budget was the sound. You must invest in good quality of sound. Another big expense was the transferring of the film.

**MN:** The first day we did stunts. This wasn't the smartest thing to do. I ended up falling and cutting my hand. Also, have everything as prepared as you can. Have it all mapped out. Use storyboards.

**What was acting in your own film like?**

**PI:** Wearing the two hats (director and actor) was tough. You know what your character is thinking and feeling, but then there's this other voice coming in saying, I wonder how this shot looks? I felt that my performance was divided a bit. I found it hard to watch myself on the screen when we screened the film.

**MN:** Acting in my own film was difficult. You have to give up the other hats you're wearing and just be the actor. It's difficult because your mind is on a thousand other things.

**You've finished shooting the film, what next?**

**PI:** We sent the film out to be developed as we went along. Next you transfer it to video. Then it goes into the computer, and that's where you start the editing. Juli was the main editor. You develop a rough cut and see if you like that. Then another rough cut, then another. Next you put your sound in, and a musical score. We promoted it and started showing it around. We had a showing at the Knitting Factory here in New York.

**MN:** After the shoot, our director did the editing of the film. We saved a lot of money on editing because he had access to editing equipment. He made up a rough cut and then we all worked with him editing the next cut. Next we did some looping and voice-over work. He put some nice titles on it and then packaging and then we were through.

**How do you find out about and enter your film in the film festivals?**

**PI:** There's a book of all the festivals and you pick which ones are right for your film. The film is showing right now in the Chicago festival. The fees for the festivals are $25–$50 [Sundance is $50]. You send a press kit with your video and hope for the best. We went to the New York Underground festival, and one in New Jersey. The festivals are really a source of promotion for your film. You don't have to be at the festival where your film is showing. About 70 percent of people whose films are showing aren't at the actual festival. It helps to be there and network with people.

For me, as an actor, making a film was a good way to promote my acting career. First, I postcarded people letting them know that I made a film and that it's in a festival. Next I offered to send copies to casting directors. I've actually gotten work from several casting directors who saw my movie. Also, I can give copies of the film to anyone who wants to see my acting work.

**MN:** We won't be entering the pilot in any festivals but we're going to make a feature (based on the pilot), and that we will enter in the festivals. We will be sending this pilot around and hopefully someone will be interested.

**Any advice that you might have for actors thinking about making their own movies?**

**PI:** I suggest that you go with professional actors on your film. Hiring friends can create all kinds of problems [even if they are also actors]. As a producer I learned to be diplomatic with the actors and crew if a problem came up. That's something you don't have to deal with when you're just the actor in a movie. I did a two hundred–piece mailing to casting directors and agents after the movie [was completed] inviting them to the New York festival. It ended up getting me some auditions and jobs.

**MN:** Always allow double the amount of time you thought you needed for a shoot. If you think it'll take an hour, give yourself two hours. There's always something that goes awry.

If you're thinking of making a TV pilot as we did, and it doesn't get picked up, there's nowhere else for the pilot to go. Whereas if you make a feature film [which can potentially be the first episode of a future series], you can have two successes [feature film and TV pilot]. By making a feature film, there are still ways to make your money back. With making just a TV pilot, the odds aren't in your favor. You'd do better making a feature.

Rather than producing an Off-Broadway play, you can invest that same money into making a short film, probably with better results. A film is something permanent that you can have. A play will end and that's it.

# Artists' Support Organizations

**A**s most actors have learned, money is not an easy thing to come by in promoting and developing your acting career. Fortunately there are organizations that assist actors, performance artists, and theater companies to lighten their loads.

### Helping You Help Yourself

Most of these organizations are not-for-profit groups that help performers with everything from getting grants to press coverage to rehearsal space to all sorts of technical assistance. I am listing just a few New York City–based organizations. There are many more all over the country.

**Dance Theater Workshop**
**219 West Nineteenth Street**
**New York, NY 10011**
**(212) 691-6500**
Dance Theater Workshop (DTW) is a not-for-profit, community-based organization that provides artist-sponsorship programs and

production facilities as well as a broad spectrum of administrative, promotional, and technical services to the community of independent artists in New York and across the country. Such notable artists as Whoopi Goldberg, Bill Irwin, and Paul Zaloom (to name just a very few) found an early artistic home at Dance Theater Workshop. The workshop's mission is "to identify and nurture emerging and maturing contemporary artists working in diverse cultural contexts; to stimulate and develop a broader audience for these artists and their work; and to create opportunities within which these artists can create by providing an interactive community laboratory for the working imagination and its essential, practical application to the world that surrounds us."

Founded in 1965 by Jeff Duncan, Art Bauman, and Jack Moore, DTW is a multifaceted organization devoted to developing programs and resources that help independent artists grow professionally while increasing the public's involvement in the arts. Dance Theater Workshop is one of the country's most active producers of new talent.

Each member receives a membership kit which helps artists plan and execute performances. The kit helps the performer keep track of preproduction deadlines, schedules, and procedures, as well as more general administrative and technical needs. Members also receive a press reference kit, which includes updated press lists, information on what to include in a press release, and general specifications on what makes a useful press photograph. The kit even includes press label sets organized by publication deadlines for your press release mailings. DTW has a complete mailing preparation service (which includes labeling, bundling and sorting, bagging, and post-office delivery) that enables performers to save on postage costs by using DTW's nonprofit bulk-mail permit.

Another service that Dance Theater Workshop provides is a low-cost video service that includes recording, postproduction, and viewing facilities. And finally, DTW offers financial assistance for performers through different grants and funds.

**Circum-Arts**
**31 West Twenty-first Street, Third floor**
**New York, NY 10010**
**(212) 675-9650; fax (212) 675-9657**

Circum-Arts is a not-for-profit arts administration organization that assists and encourages performing artists. Its goal is to provide a complete structure of administrative, technical, and management resources that are accessible and affordable to individual artists and emerging companies. The organization was created in 1973 and presently serves more than two hundred artists. Aside from helping its own members, it assists hundreds of additional artists that aren't members.

Circum-Arts helps artists find funding and work as a sponsorship organization, providing artists with access to funding from government, corporate, and foundation sources. Circum-Arts also allows the artist's audience and supporters to receive a tax deduction when donating funds to the artist.

The organization strives to perform all its services to artists at a minimum cost, allowing artists to pay as they go rather than requiring retainers or deposits. If you've started a theater company and work with Circum-Arts, it can extend the privilege of nonprofit status under its umbrella. Circum-Arts even provides a health insurance plan for its members.

**The Field**
**161 Sixth Avenue**
**New York, NY 10013**
**(212) 691-6969; fax (212) 255-2053**

The Field was created to help independent artists continue to make art. It offers three areas to cover artists' needs. These include:

- *Art-based programs.* These programs focus on aesthetic development and refinement. In a ten-week program, artists present their work-in-progress to their peers and receive feedback as the work develops. Artists can expect to find out how their work is affecting an audience before putting it up in front of the public.
- *Career-based programs.* These programs foster professional growth and opportunity. These services help artists to find

better ways to produce their work. The Field offers a ten-hour intensive grant and resource development workshop ($60–$80), as well as low-cost individual consultations in grant writing and fund-raising.

- *Exploration-based programs.* The Independent Artist Challenge Program helps artists to take their next career steps. This program helps artists with personal management strategies and cooperative promotional work, and to discover new sources for earned income. To help realize their solutions, each participant receives $1,000 for their group project and $250 for think-tank participation.

The Field programs have initiated sites in Atlanta, Chicago, Dallas, Houston, Miami, Philadelphia, San Francisco, Seattle, Toronto, and Washington D.C., with additional sites joining the network each year.

**Franklin Furnace**
**112 Franklin Street**
**New York, NY 10013-2980**
**(212) 925-4671; fax (212) 925-0903**

Franklin Furnace was founded twenty years ago by Martha Wilson as a place for avant-garde and performance artists to develop their projects. It offers these services to artists:

- Sequential Arts for Kids places professional artists in the New York City public school system.
- Franklin Furnace Fund for Performance Art presents performance art, both live and cybercast through the Internet.
- Fund for Performance Art, which is supported by the Jerome Foundation and the Joyce Mertz-Gilmore Foundation. Franklin Furnace awards grants of $2,000–$5,000 to emerging artists, allowing them to produce their work anywhere in New York State.

# Creating Your Own Theater Company

**T**he Group Theater was one of the most famous instances where actors, writers, and directors got together for a common cause— to make great theater. Over the decades there have been many other famous American acting companies all wanting to make their imprints. Aside from artistic reasons, some theater companies are created for political or social reasons.

### Banding Together with a Common Vision

There are several types of theater companies: the nonprofit companies, the commercial ones, and the actors' collectives (where actors pay a monthly fee).

Creating a theater company is a time-consuming and complex process. The group must write a mission statement stating why they've banded together, what their goals are, and what they hope to attain. Rules and goals must be set. Leaders and committees must be created to handle the day-to-day work.

Before the first show opens, there will be a great deal of preliminary work. It could take many months or even years before that first show. The potential play must be read and decided upon, money must be raised, a theater must be found, etc.

Being a member of a theater company is not for everyone. There is a great deal of tedious groundwork. But the idea of producing a successful company-generated show and being a member of an "artistic family" can be very rewarding.

### Theater Company Interviews

JOE STERN (**JS**) is the owner and artistic director of the Mattrix Theater, a Los Angeles theater company that has received the Drama Critics Circle Award for Best Production for an unprecedented four years in a row (every year that the company has been in existence). A former actor, Stern and acting pal William Devane purchased the Mattrix Theater in the late 1970s. In 1980 he became the sole owner of the theater. In the last twenty years his productions have earned 150 theater awards including 30 Los Angeles Drama Critics Circle Awards, 103 *Drama-Logue* Awards, 30 *LA Weekly* Awards, and 19 other awards from the L.A. Drama Critics Circle.

BOB LUPONE (**BL**) founded the MCC Theater with co-artistic director Bernard Telsey. MCC Theater is presently celebrating its twelfth season as a not-for-profit theater company. Inspired by the Shakespearean tradition of the actor-manager, the directors are intent upon redefining the experience of developing and producing plays in New York City. Representative productions include *Girl Gone* by Jacquelyn Rheingold (winner of the Roger L. Stevens Incentive Awards), *Beirut* (six *Drama-Logue* Awards; presented as an HBO movie entitled *Daybreak*), Terence McNally's *Prelude and Liebestod,* and Peter Hedges's *Good As New.* MCC was the recipient of *Encore* magazine's 1995–96 "Taking Off" award for Outstanding Theater Company. Its production of Russell Lee's *Nixon's Nixon* received two Outer Critics Circle nominations and the John Gassner Playwriting Award. Their production of Tim Blake Nelson's *The Grey Zone* garnered the playwright an *Encore* magazine "Taking Off" award for Outstanding Playwriting as well as an Obie Award for best new playwright (also a *Village Voice* Obie to director Douglas Hughes).

SETH BARRISH (**SB**) is the artistic director of the Barrow Group, a fifteen-member ensemble of actors, directors, and designers. Last year they coproduced the highly acclaimed production of *Old Wicked Songs*, which later on moved to the Promenade Theatre for a successful commercial run. They received considerable attention for their productions of *Lonely Planet* by Steven Dietz (later coproduced Off Broadway with the Circle Rep. Company). Last year the Barrow Group received a Drama Desk Award for best Off-off Broadway ensemble.

MICHAEL WARREN POWELL (**MP**) is the artistic director of the Lab Theater Company (formerly artistic director of Circle Rep. Lab). Among the three hundred artists involved in this company are Giancarlo Esposito, Barnard Hughes, Bill Fichtner, John Seitz, Craig Lucas, Joe Pintauro, Lanford Wilson, William M. Hoffman, Terence McNally, Johnathan Hogan, Marshal W. Mason, and William Esper.

---

**Whose idea was it to start this company? What were the reasons behind starting a new theater company? What were your goals?**

**JS:** Andrew Robinson, Larry Pressman, and Penny Fuller were three of the principal actors who started this company. The founding members also included Robin Gammel, Tony Giordano, Charles Hallahan, Mary Joan Nigro, and Cotter Smith. The Mattrix Theater has always existed. It was called Actors for Themselves. It did a couple of plays a year. We decided to move it into a different permutation in 1993 and call it the Mattrix Theater. Basically, the impetus was for fiscal and artistic reasons. Simply, actors, as we know, just can't afford to do theater anymore.

The idea was to double-cast every role. With understudies the drop in skill level is tremendous. It always cheated the production and the audience. The idea was to maintain the quality of the productions. With double-casting all the actors, both casts would rehearse with the director at the same time. One actor would be in the audience and the other actor would be onstage. Then they'd alternate. It's as if the fictional character has two heads.

The reason for starting the company was to get a group of actors together to form a collective. The goal simply was to get actors to return to the theater who previously could not afford to do it. Another goal was to challenge both the actor and the audience. Each play we did had a different style. The American actor has become an endangered species because he can't afford to make a living anymore. And more and more are quitting the business after forty. The idea of the company was to be role models for younger actors like it was when I was younger. Younger actors working with older ones could learn as they worked. This country really doesn't support the arts. Artists will always create their own environment.

**BL:** I was teaching acting to eight students and we all got bored after two years. We liked each other and wanted to stay together so the next logical step was to form a theater company. The tradition was the Shakespearean actor-manager idea where we'd read plays every week together and then try to formulate a theater. I was trying to find some theater roots for myself after working in this town for a number of years. I, personally, was in some ways confused. I followed along with Bernie's (Telsey) idea of starting a theater company, which was something he'd always wanted to do. Bernie, aside from being a theater major at NYU, was also a theater administration major. From 1983–86 we tried a for-profit company. We were going to work on new plays and then sell them at backers' auditions to producers. Then we'd go back to the studio and work on new plays. We did eventually get options for two Broadway plays. But the money wasn't enough to keep us afloat. Bernie convinced us that the best way to go on was to go nonprofit. For a while we were at the Nat Horne Theater on Theater Row doing our one-acts, and then eventually we got our own space.

**SB:** It was my and Nate Harvery's idea. It was a combination of factors. We were a group of actors looking for a place to be able to play and work in a way that was fun for us. We were young, just going out in the real world to work in various places. A lot of times it was frustrating for different reasons. We had complaints about the directors we'd work with, the plays, whatever. We had become fascinated with an acting style that was particularly "documentary-esque," ultra-real. We didn't feel that we were expert at it, but it did interest us. Our main goal in acting was that the audience lose sight that they were watching an actor and feel like they were in a room with a real person. We didn't plan on producing originally, it just worked out that way.

**MP:** In this case we had a company without a home. For the previous ten years the company existed as a laboratory for a larger theater company. When the mother company (Circle Rep. Theater) ceased to exist, a large group of actors, designers, directors, writers, and stage managers found themselves with a common bond and a desire to continue working together. This company exists through the belief of its membership, which is huge. About 150 actors, 40 directors, 50 writers, and several designers and stage managers. At the moment, we have a volunteer staff and are plunging ahead. Our goal is to develop new plays, writers, actors, and directors and to present these developed works to the public. The Lab is my idea, strongly suggested by the disenfranchised artists of the Circle Repertory Company.

**What problems did you face originally? How did you eventually overcome them (if you did)?**

**JS:** We didn't want this to be something competitive. When you have this double-casting, it can become that. We still have two opening nights but in the beginning the papers reviewed both nights. As the novelty wore off there were less and less double reviews and more and more single reviews. Actors, by the flip of a coin, would be reviewed. So one actor would be reviewed and the other not.

The way the company originated was that I invited eighty or ninety actors that I worked with over the years to a reading of a play. Then we had discussion afterward about the play and whether we felt this system could work. I took the information from that meeting and then selected the first play. Another way we avoided competitiveness between actors was to cast two very different types for each role. In our first play, *The Tavern*, Cotter Smith and Robin Gammel played the same role. Both are extremely different types. With this technique we proved that there's more than one way to tell the truth. We'd have symposiums after each production with the actors and discuss what we could and couldn't improve. We discovered that this technique was most difficult on the directors. Directors had to carry the load. We started with four weeks of rehearsals and ended with six weeks. We started with two weeks of previews and then went to three weeks. We didn't want to shortchange the audience in terms of the critics and everything else. The great thing about Los Angeles theater is that because there's not really a contract, you have enough flexibility to expand the time to fit the work.

**BL:** Clarity—about what an artistic mission is, funding, overcoming ignorance, both artistically and financially, and working out the dynamic of relationships. An organization has many growth processes. You start off with enthusiasm and innocence, and then you work toward survival, and then as you become more professional, volunteers fall by the wayside so you have to hire a staff. It's all an evolution.

Bottom line—long hours, grit, and determination! How do you overcome the problems? With passion and belief in the theater. Always keeping in mind the importance and nobility of it.

**SB:** Raising money was the first major hurdle we came to. We were artists and we had to learn about the business side of the business. We hooked up with people who were adept at doing this type of work. A lot of it we just learned while doing, making horrible mistakes along the way, but always learning and getting better at it.

**MP:** Sadly, it seems all theater companies' problems are money. I have an enormous wealth of talent in my ensemble, countless projects worthy of production, a teaching staff, and still no home to house it or major funding to staff it. We have overcome the lack of money by accepting free space from the New York community and producing marathons of brilliant work from this company.

**What was your first public production? How did it go? What lessons did you learn from doing that production?**

**JS:** It was *The Tavern,* our biggest success. Tony Giordano, the director, had suggested the play. He had done it twice in the regions. It was nominated for seven or eight L.A. Drama Critics Circle Awards and it won for best play. It went incredibly well, was a huge hit. We learned that we needed more time to rehearse, that we needed most of the actors at all the rehearsals as much as possible. Especially at the beginning of the rehearsal of a play.

**BL:** It was the *Class One-Acts*, in 1986. We really didn't know what we were doing back then. One thing we learned though was the amount of work it takes to put on a production. Also the fragility to corralling all the creative talents along with your own ignorance toward a united vision.

**SB:** The first thing we did was a one-night event at the Perry Street Theater. We raised $7,000 that night. We did the public premiere of some of Joe Pintauro's plays. In some ways it went very well; in others, not. We put a ton of attention into the artistic side. We invited prospective board members. The evening was successful in that we got an instant board of directors. We were thrilled that we were able to pull it off. We learned about the process of working with each other and designers in a production mode. The main thing we learned was that it was possible to do.

**MP:** *All Day Sucker* at Circle in the Square Downtown. We did forty-five short plays in twelve hours. It was an enormous success; lines around the block all day. It is now an annual event having completed *All Day Sucker II* and planning *All Day Sucker III*. We produced *Scaring the Fish* by Ben Bettenbender at the Magic Theater in San Francisco. We produced Clarke Middleton's *Miracle Mile* at Theater Row Theater, and a coproduction of *The Quick Change Room* by Nigel Jackson, directed by Orson Bean, at the Intar Theater. We plan to accept the invitation of the West Bank Theater Cafe for month-long residencies. Last November and April we presented over 100 plays there. And in the 1996–97 season, we presented 222 new plays.

### What are the advantages of being part of an artist-created theater company? Any disadvantages?

**JS:** The major thing is empowerment. It always has been. The actor has always been a third-class citizen up until the last fifteen years. He never directed or produced, he just acted. The actor has to be a producer to facilitate his own employment. That's been the major part of the explosion in L.A. with some 1,200 productions a year mostly actor driven. The main disadvantage is monetary. You don't get any grants. One thing to our advantage is that I own the building. The three years that I worked on *Law and Order*, I rented the building out and the money that I made was the seed money for the company. It's a nonprofit company.

**BL:** Shorthand and communication are a couple of the advantages. Working with other like minds toward a common vision is very rewarding, very satisfying. Some of the disadvantages are the difficulties you encounter in fund-raising, professional management of an office, marketing, getting an audience, advertising. The list goes on.

**SB:** The advantages are you quickly learn there are no excuses. You get a constant reality litmus test about how you're doing. It's easy to blame the world and not really grow. Also, you develop a working shorthand with people so that certain kinds of things can happen quickly. There's a possibility for a kind of aesthetic that everybody shares. The disadvantages are you attach yourself to a family that's bound to be dysfunctional. As people grow, their agendas change and you sometimes have to compromise or separate.

**MP:** My choices of what we do is directly suggested by the works and wishes of the membership. Since their labor will make the projects happen, their ownership is necessary. An artist-generated company will probably always lack business expertise. So you might say the advantages and disadvantages are exactly the same. The advantage is that it's artist generated, the disadvantage is that it's artist generated.

**What advice do you have for other actors wanting to start their own company?**

**JS:** What I did was that I got all my friends, who I had worked with and trusted and had prior relationships with, together. These were all wonderful actors. I recommend other actors wanting to start their own company to do the same thing. Then you must eliminate those people with personal agendas. You must be able to depend on every person in your company. They must have character. There's very little money or contractual obligations so you must be certain that they're team players. You must all have a very like mind to collaborate. Intuitively, you must know who will be able to work well in such a close collaboration as a theater company. There are two things that destroy all companies. A cancer from within because of bad behavior, bad character, and the inability to be part of a team, and to a certain degree, expansion. Also don't compromise the art of what you're doing by allowing people who aren't gifted to enter the company by volunteerism.

**BL:** If you want to start a theater company so you can act, don't do it. If you want to start a theater company so you can say something about the world we live in, that's a good reason. Involving myself with this theater has taught me a lot about interpersonal relationships, and that has impacted on me as an actor. I've had to talk with press people, public relations people, even with fellow employees. By and large it's been immensely rewarding.

**SB:** Terence McNally's advice to me about creating my own theater company was, Be patient. It's a long haul. One other thing I've learned, the hard way, was someone really has to be in charge. It makes things much easier. Originally, we started off as a democracy, but eventually we learned that a group functions best with a leader.

**MP:** My advice for actors wanting to start their own company is, Just do it! Don't wait around to be selected by the whimsies of commercial producers. Over ten years ago I gave this advice to the actors who became the Barrow Group. And they have made a respected company whose productions are of consistent high quality, and the level of acting is superb. The artists who make theater instead of waiting to be discovered are an inspiration. The creative energy for making your own theater is infectious. Let's inspire each other. Patience is necessary; however, waiting for someone else to make it happen can leave you empty. Creating theater is very fulfilling for the artist and for the audience.

# CHAPTER 28

# Casting Directors

In some of the talent agents' interviews, the agents referred to themselves as the "sellers." In the entertainment industry, the casting directors are the "buyers." It is their job to arrange auditions so that actors can meet with directors, producers, and sometimes writers, for a particular project. The director and the producer depend on the casting director for their contacts and knowledge of the available talent pool. The casting director often advises the director or producer as to an actor's potential for a particular role.

### What They Do

It is the casting director's job to understand the casting needs of whatever project it is that he's working on. If it's a movie or play, he must read the script and then consult with the writer, director, and/or producer as to what types they're seeking for each of the roles. The casting director will contact talent agents to discuss which of their clients might be right for a role. For film and TV projects, the casting director contacts the daily breakdown services, which send out their casting needs to agents every day.

Casting directors work in one of several categories (sometimes overlapping):

- *Advertising agency casting directors* work for a particular advertising agency. They cast actors in TV commercials, radio spots, voice-overs, and sometimes print work.
- *Network casting directors* (daytime and prime time) work for a particular TV network. They oversee all casting for the shows on their network. They generally are concerned with the casting of the stars and up-and-coming stars for their network's shows.
- *Independent casting directors* work as freelancers in commercials, movies, and theater. In some cases they have their own offices.
- *Soap opera casting directors* are hired to cast contract roles as well as day players for their particular shows. They are also known as daytime casting directors. Their casting assistants cast the under-fives as well as extras.

### Daytime Casting Directors

There presently are eleven daytime serials. Six of them shoot in Los Angeles and five in New York City. The New York shows are:

- *All My Children.* Casting director: Judy Blye-Wilson; Under-fives and extras: Elias Tray
- *Another World.* Casting director: Jimmy Bohr; Under-fives and extras: Elizabeth Wilson
- *As the World Turns.* Casting director: Vince Liebhart; Under-fives and extras: Tom Alberg
- *Guiding Light.* Casting director: Glenn Daniels; Under-fives and extras: Melanie Haseltine
- *One Life to Live.* Casting Director: Sonia Nikore; Under-fives and extras: Victoria Visgilio

The Los Angeles shows are:

- *The Bold and the Beautiful.* Casting director: Christy Dooley
- *Days of Our Lives.* Casting director: Fran Bascom
- *General Hospital.* Casting director: Mark Teschner
- *Sunset Beach.* Casting directors: Melinda Gartzman and Lisa Booth; Assistant casting director: Peggy Illman

- *The Young and the Restless*. Casting director: Meryl O'Loughlin; Associate casting director: Gail Camacho
- *Port Charles*. Casting director: Mark Teschner

### Interviews with Daytime Casting Directors

MARK TESCHNER (**MT**) has been the casting director for *General Hospital* since 1989. He also casts the daytime show *Port Charles*. He has been an independent casting director for fourteen years. *Rolling Stone* magazine described him as "an actor's casting director." For his work on *General Hospital* he has received four Artios Award nominations for Outstanding Achievement in Soaps Casting. Teschner is on the Board of Governors for the Academy of Television Arts and Sciences and is also the vice president of the Casting Society of America.

JIMMY BOHR (**JB**) casts contract roles and principal day players for *Another World*. He is also a professional director. His directing credits include the original productions of *Beirut* as well as *Romeo and Juliet* at the New Jersey Shakespeare Festival, and productions at the Roundabout Theater, MCC, as well as other regional and Off-Broadway theaters.

ELIAS TRAY (**ET**) has been the associate casting director at *All My Children* for five years. He was formerly the assistant casting director at Grey Advertising. He received his acting training at NYU.

VINCE LIEBHART (**VL**) casts principal and contract players for *As the World Turns*. He also cast the Off-Broadway show *Stomp* (three companies). He's worked with David Gordon on his piece *The Mysteries and What's So Funny?*, which was done at Serious Fun and at the Joyce Theater. It won an Obie and a Bessie. He has also worked with Philip Glass.

FRAN BASCOM (**FB**) is currently casting *Days of Our Lives*. Prior to that she cast *Designing Women, Evening Shade, Hearts of Fire, Women of the House,* and *Lou Grant.*

*Note: You'll notice that in some cases the casting directors' answers to a particular question are the same. Such repetition is a pretty good indication that the advice should be taken to heart.*

**What do you look at first on an actor's headshot?**

**MT:** I want to see what that person is about, not what that person is trying to be. A good headshot should look like an actor at her best as opposed to how she would like to look. It's something in the eyes, something in the look. It's not about selling, it's about being. The photo should capture something in that actor that makes me want to meet her.

**JB:** Most importantly, it should look like the person. I look for someone who looks very much alive, very relaxed, essentially kind of neutral. If it's a picture with a "bitchy" attitude, then one assumes that that's all you can do. I look for something open, honest, natural, and with some life to it.

**ET:** What I like is the old-fashioned shot, the close-up of the face. I'm not big on the three-quarter because I really like to see if there is some sort of expression, if there's something special. I want to see if they've captured a certain feeling about themselves that they're able to convey to me through the picture.

**VL:** It really depends on what I'm looking for. I look for some sort of vitality. But I wouldn't encourage people to do something really goofy. I've seen effective headshots that clearly express the actor's individual personality without being too splashy.

**FB:** Trained actors seem to come across better in their photos than inexperienced ones. Perhaps it's their confidence that's captured. I don't feel actors need three-quarter shots or full-length shots, although I must admit I've seen some very good ones.

**What do you look for on an actor's résumé?**

**MT:** I'm partial to theater. What plays they've been in, where they've worked, what regional theater, what roles they've played—all of that interests me. The training is also very important. Particularly for young actors who haven't worked much yet, I want to know if they're presently studying and with which teacher.

**JB:** I'm particularly interested in training. I'm also interested in the kind of work someone has done. I like to see the quality of the kind of work that's been done. "Interesting work begets interesting work"; and certainly training helps with that. I look at the kind of theaters or the films or television shows the actor has done. I hate to see plays listed and not know where they were done. *The Importance of Being Earnest* at the Guthrie is a little different than *The Importance of Being Earnest* at the Huntsville Little Theater. Not that I'm making a judgment about that or that there couldn't have been a good production there. But where you've worked, the television shows, films, the nature of the work is determined by the show itself. This includes the theaters, directors, playwrights. If an actor doesn't have much experience, I just focus on the training.

**ET:** I look for lots of strong stage and regional credits. If the actor is a member of Actors Equity, I want to see if he got in because he worked in strong Equity theaters or because he was Equity eligible and did some extra work and just paid to join. I was previously an actor so I know (and auditioned for) a lot of the small theaters around the country. I feel that by now I sort of know the better LORT (League of Regional Theaters) theaters.

**VL:** I always look for training.

**FB:** Education and training is of significance to me. That's what I glance at first.

**How do you suggest actors make themselves known to you? What do you recommend they don't do?**

**MT:** I strongly believe that you can't make someone see you. Obviously an agent helps, but many actors do get to meet casting directors without them. Actors must constantly create work for themselves. They should always challenge themselves and try to work in a venue where they can be seen. I don't believe in gimmicks. I don't like receiving unsolicited phone calls. Actors should not send photos and résumés week after week. You should send a photo and résumé and then follow up a month or so later with a postcard letting me know what you're up to. Maybe a new photo six months after that. I want an actor who's confident in his work as well as with who he is as a person.

**JB:** Gimmicks of any kind I think are foolish. The only real measure of an actor is how he acts, period! It's much more exciting for me when I get to know someone I don't know by seeing them onstage or in a film. I don't want or appreciate gifts from people I don't know solely to get me to notice their résumés.

**ET:** Originally they should send in their eight-by-tens. I look at every eight-by-ten I get. The cover letter is very important. It tells me a little bit about who you are. You might capture something about yourself that I wasn't aware of by just looking at your photo and résumé. I receive up to three hundred pictures a day. From those three hundred, I may hold on to ten or twenty to call in for future generals. Sending me a postcard when I haven't met you is silly. I like to know if you're in a showcase, if you've booked something—just generally what's up. Actors should not telephone if I don't know who they are or if I haven't put a call out to them. Don't send presents. Presents make me feel like I'm being paid off to cast or meet you.

**VL:** Don't call me! Pictures and résumés initially. Notification of any plays if you're in any episodic work. Don't drop by!

**FB:** If an actor is in a play, I suggest he send me a flier or phone and leave the information with my assistant. I go to a great deal of theater. I am inundated with pictures and résumés, and it's impossible to give each one the attention it may deserve. I feel an actor should not make a nuisance of himself by phoning incessantly.

**What determines whether you'll see an actor in a show or not?**

**MT:** There's not one thing. It's a random selection process. An actor whose work has intrigued me and I want to see more of, a play that I want to see, a theater company, all of these things. I will go anywhere to see a play. You always want to make sure the flier is professional looking. I personally prefer to see a play that has more actors in it rather than less. I cast a lot of my day players from people I see in the theater.

**JB:** I like to see good theater, period. If the show is bad, don't expect me to come see it even if you're giving a really good performance. I much prefer to see real theater than to see "scene nights." I'll go anywhere if it's something good. The reputation of the actors, the theater, the playwright, the directors, reviews, word of mouth—all inform me as to what the production might be like.

**ET:** The theater company that she's working with. There are many fine theater companies in this city. If someone is involved with a strong theater company where I've found many talented actors that I've booked on the show, then obviously I'm going to be more inclined to go to that showcase. The other thing that's very important is the location and the time. If I'm invited to two interesting showcases (or shows) and one is on theater row and one is way downtown, I'll probably go to the midtown show. Another consideration is time. Industry performances (usually 6:30 or 7:00 P.M.) are really a plus for me. I'm not going to the theater to be entertained; I'm going to work.

**VL:** If I like the play, if I've heard that the showcase is good, if my interest is sparked by the actor, the writing, whatever.

**FB:** My availability. I try to see several actors in a play. A one-man show is not as rewarding for me. I don't go to be entertained. I go to see the actors. Location of a theater is also a factor, since it is virtually impossible at the end of a workday to get to a theater on the other side of town.

### Any specific actor do's and don'ts?

**MT:** I respond well to confidence—not arrogance. I respond to an actor who has a strong sense of who she is—a presence—and, of course, to good work. I don't respond well to actors who emanate a neediness, who telegraph that they need the job. If an actor isn't confident in her work, or at peace with who she is, then she needs to work on that to succeed in this business.

**JB:** I look for artistic choices that actors make. As I said, the only thing that gets my attention is good work. I feel I'm very sympathetic to actors; I understand the difficulties.

**ET:** Trust. If someone agrees to work a job, I expect her to show up. Of course, if she gets a major film or a big commercial, I'm very understanding and hope we can work it out. But if someone's doing a recurring role, and by her not showing up a direct pickup will be ruined, the show is unhappy and so am I. To me this is breaking a contract. Also there are skills. If you claim you have the ability to perform a skill for a particular role, I expect that to be true. Please don't lie. Next there's the guilt thing. I really don't like actors writing things like, Why aren't you using me anymore? Have I done something wrong? Actors should not personalize our jobs. Actors who I book represent me on the set. I expect them to be on time and I expect not to get complaints about them. Being on a soap set is not the time to try to meet the stars or to network with other actors. Also, actors should not visit my office uninvited (unless I've told them it's okay to do so). There's a big sign down by my casting office requesting actors not to bother us while we are working, yet I can't tell you how many do. I watch the show all day on the monitor so I know what's going on.

**VL:** I really expect an actor to be prepared. I don't expect a scene to be memorized for an audition, but I do want the actor to have given it some real thought. Don't make apologies. I'm open to any questions that actors may have at the audition. Actually, one thing that really bothers me: I always ask, "Do you have any questions?" I don't mind if they don't have any questions and just want to do the scene. But sometimes you just feel that they're searching for something to say because you've asked that question. Another pet peeve is when an actor gets my number and calls and asks, "Can you give me your address? I want to send a picture and résumé." If every actor did that, I'd never get any work done.

**FB:** My main pet peeve is to have actors arrive for auditions without a picture and résumé. This happens frequently and it makes me angry. I don't mind as much when they come without a photo, for whatever reason, but I do mind not having a résumé to refer to. The whole interview becomes difficult to conduct.

### When interviewing actors, what do you look for?

**MT:** I look at their energy, their sensibility, their sense of themselves. I want to feel that they're comfortable dealing with me. I rarely do generals because they don't tell me that much about the actor's talents.

**JB:** I do general interviews all the time. I'm not "looking for" anything. I'm essentially very open to whatever it is they want to give me. In an interview, I want to know about your work, how you deal with your career, what work you like, how you approach your work. I want to know what kind of artist you are, and what that means to you. I don't particularly want to know about your personal life. I want to know about your professional life. I think it's important to be able to talk about the work you've been doing, to be able to talk about the work you'd like to do. And I don't just mean about a good job that makes me a lot of money. "My favorite role was this, and this is why. The best artistic experience I ever had was this, because. . . ."

**ET:** Many actors become nervous at interviews. That's to be expected and it's okay. I like to see someone who has a strong sense of himself, a sense of confidence, from the minute he enters the door. I like to feel that he's solid, trustworthy. I want to feel that once he's up on the set, he'll be reliable and professional.

**VL:** I rarely have general interviews, but when I do, I look for some sense of personality. The interview is in the actor's court a lot. What I look for is basically what can they bring to the show?

**FB:** An outgoing personality is helpful. It makes the interview pleasant to conduct and one gets to know and remember that particular actor when a role comes up. Actors who contribute nothing to the conversation and give one-word answers will not make a lasting impression. Good grooming and a nice appearance are also vital.

### When auditioning actors, what do you look for?

**MT:** Talent, first. Craft, ability, someone that can take what's on that page and find a way to own it. You must fit the concept, the sensibility of the role. Also I look for a certain presence, a charisma. Sometimes an actor comes in and even though she is a bit uneven in her craft, there's something compelling about her. She has a strong presence.

**JB:** Talent! Strong, clear choices, command of the language. There are so many actors, who, when auditioning for daytime, think they don't have to talk. A lot of actors who audition for daytime think you can mumble—that's wrong! I can't tell you how many actors mumble through an audition. I want to say, I can't hear you! Command of the language is imperative no matter what medium of acting you're in. I also look for a strong emotional availability at the audition.

**ET:** I call many actors in after I've seen them in a show so I know something about their talents and abilities. At my office audition, however, I look to see if, first, they understand the role I'm reading them for. Also what's important for me is to see if actors can make adjustments. I will give them direction and I want to see if they can apply it. It's very important in this medium that they can make the adjustment without going through a process that's too lengthy.

**VL:** Because of the nature of daytime, I look for personality. I look for it to be part of what they've brought to the scene. In daytime, actors don't get a lot of input, so actors must have the ability to create something with the scene.

**FB:** I hope actors will have good cold-reading abilities. I also expect them to be able to make adjustments at the audition. If the actor gives a good audition, you always remember him if not for this role but certainly for parts in the future. If he doesn't have the right look, he won't get the job no matter how good his audition is.

**How do you prefer actors maintain contact with your office? How often?**

**MT:** Every so often an actor can send me a note or postcard letting me know what she's up to. Use the postcard as an opportunity to let me know what you've been doing. A generic hello is fine every couple of months.

**FB:** If I don't know you, there's no reason to bombard me daily with pictures or postcards. A postcard tells me nothing about you. If we know each other, then remain in contact when you have something to tell me—when you're in a show or film, or on TV. I tend not to forget people.

**ET:** I love to get postcards from actors I know. I want to know what you're doing, if you're in something, if you're going on vacation for two months, if you just got the European tour of *Cats*, whatever. I like to hear that actors are working. Another reason (for the card updates) is I won't put out calls to you if you're not available. If you're just checking in, a postcard every six weeks is enough.

**VL:** Only contact me when there's something new or if you're in a show. I discard pictures of people I don't know unless there's some unique skill on their résumé that I might need. If there's a picture and résumé with a lot of stuff on it, I might keep it because I feel that perhaps this is an actor I should know.

**FB:** Just send a postcard from time to time updating your activities.

**If you had just one tip (any advice) to give to actors regarding their careers, what would it be?**

**MT:** You can't sit back and wait for your career to happen. As a fellow casting director once said, "Each actor is president of his own company. He has to do something actively every day for the benefit of his company."

The other thing—love to act. Do it because you love it and not for any other reason. All the rest is illusive. Stardom, financial success are all just by-products. An actor has only two things—her talent and her dignity.

**JB:** Work as much as you can. I think that those people who spend most of their lives marketing themselves are not real actors. If you're good you're going to be noticed.

**ET:** Don't start sending out pictures and résumés until you're ready, really ready! Don't send them out until you feel totally capable and ready to handle the workload that a daytime actor must face. First impressions are very important in this business. If you're not ready yet, not trained enough, that will show at the audition. How many times do you get to make a good first impression?

**VL:** One thing that I feel is that schools and conservatories do not prepare actors for this profession. Julliard and Yale should be teaching the business of acting. When actors come to New York, they do have to make a living. Many actors don't even know what an agent or manager does.

**FB:** Get together with your fellow actors and work on scenes. Keep on studying. Just keep going. Don't give up.

### Interviews with Casting Directors: Theater, TV, and Film

SHIRLEY RICH (**SR**) is an independent casting director. The films she has cast include: *Kramer vs. Kramer; Saturday Night Fever; Serpico; Rachel, Rachel; Taps; Three Days of the Condor;* and *Tender Mercies.* Her casting for TV includes: *American Playhouse* ("André's Mother," "Ask Me Again"), *Prince of Central Park, Ryans's Hope* (original cast). For theater, she has cast, among others: *Ballroom, Crimes of the Heart, Sly Fox* (casting director, national; consultant, Broadway), and *God's Favorite.* For Hal Prince she cast *Fiddler on the Roof,* (three companies), *Cabaret* (three companies), and *Zorba,* and she assistant cast *The King and I,* and *South Pacific.*

RISA BRAMON GARCIA (**RG**) is an independent casting director in Los Angeles. She has been directing plays for twenty-two years and casting movies for twelve. Some of the films she has cast include: *Desperately Seeking Susan, Fatal Attraction, JFK* (eight films with Oliver Stone), *Speed,* and *The Joy Luck Club.*

She feels that she is primarily a director and that casting is her "waitressing job." She will be directing a movie for MTV for Mike Newell's company.

LORI OPPENDEN (**LO**), senior vice president of Talent and Casting at NBC in Los Angeles, was a television casting director for ten years. She did the casting for such shows as *Hill Street Blues* and *Cheers*.

PETER GOLDEN (**PG**), vice president of Talent and Casting at CBS in Los Angeles, oversees the casting of series, pilots, movies of the week, and mini-series. He started out with Hughes Moss casting in New York City. Ten years ago he moved to Los Angeles to work at Universal in the casting department. Next he went to director of casting at NBC, then worked at head of casting Grant Tinker's company, GTG, then for Stephen Cannel as head of casting, and then in development for John Landis.

MARC HIRSCHFELD (**MH**) along with his partner Meg Liberman at Liberman-Hirschfeld Casting, presently casts *Seinfeld, Party of Five, The Larry Sanders Show, Grace Under Fire,* and *Third Rock From the Sun.* They did the original casting for *The Nanny, Married with Children, American Gothic,* and *Sliders,* among others.

RONNIE YESKEL (**RY**) is an independent casting director. Along with her associate Richard Hicks, she casts for film, TV, and theater. For TV, she cast three seasons of *L.A. Law* and *Dangerous Minds.* Some of the films she cast were *Pulp Fiction, Reservoir Dogs, Things to Do in Denver When You're Dead, The Long Kiss Goodbye, Hope Floats, Montana, Dr. Bean,* and *The Underneath.*

BERNIE TELSEY (**BT**) at Bernard Telsey Casting, works with Will Cantler, David Vaccari, Heidi Marshall, and Lori Saposnick, casting for film, theater, TV, and commercials. The company cast the Pulitzer- and Tony-winning musical *Rent* (original New York Company and both national companies). Other Broadway shows include: *Present Laughter, The Young Man From Atlanta,* and *The Capeman.* Films include: *A Modern Affair* and *The Peacemaker* (New York casting). TV casting includes the HBO series *The High Life.* Telsey's company also casts for Hartford Stage Company, Long Wharf Theater Company, La Jolla Playhouse, MCC Theater, and New York Theater Workshop, among others. Telsey is coexecutive of MCC Theater, producer of *Beirut, Nixon's Nixon, The Grey Zone,* and *Good As New.*

PAT MCCORKLE (**PM**) of McCorkle Casting, casts for theater, film, and TV. McCorkle Casting has been involved with such diverse projects as *A Few Good Men*, productions at the Roundabout Theater, *Ghostwriter* for TV, many of the *Lifestories* for HBO, and the *Remember WENN* series (American Movie Channel), to name just a few.

STUART HOWARD (**SH**) with Stuart Howard Associates, casts for theater, film, TV commercials, and videos. The company's first show was *La Cage Aux Folles*. "Our two favorites," says Howard, "were *Gypsy* on Broadway and *Gypsy* on television."

STANLEY SOBLE (**SS**) casts for the Center Theater Group (the Mark Taper Forum and the Ahmenson Theater) and does other freelance casting work when he's available. He cast the Los Angeles production of *Angels in America* and did half the casting of it in New York City. He also cast *Big River* and *Jelly's Last Jam* for Broadway, as well as the L.A. production of *Our Country's Good*. Another show he cast in Los Angeles, *Stand-Up Tragedy*, went to New York.

CHARLES ROSEN (**CR**) and ANNETTE KUREK (AK), are with Charles Rosen Casting, which casts for TV, voice-overs, commercials, films, and theater (including babies). "We're really trying to pick up in the legit and film area. We have an Off-Broadway show coming up called *Gender Wars*. We're doing a second summer season for Pittsburgh Light Opera. Last year we did a wonderful show called *Lucia Mad*. For San Antonio we did *Murder by Chocolate* by Joe Pintauro."

*Note: Once again, when responses to certain questions are repeated by several casting directors, take notice! It's a good indication that it's something you should or should not do.*

---

### What do you look at first in an actor's headshot?

**SR:** One thing I must mention, lately there has been a trend toward this unshaven look for men. I don't like it at all. Basically, I just want it to look like the actor, no ifs, whats, or buts.

**RG:** I look for an intensity and a focus. I want to see if the person is photogenic. I look for an intelligence in the eyes. Can the person grab me? I want to see confidence. I look for a lot of things. If I don't see everything, then I usually move on.

**LO:** I just look at it and wait for something to grab me. The eyes first. I look at all the pictures we get here (and there can be hundreds), and throw most of them away.

**PG:** Naturally, I look for something interesting in the face. There's not that much that you can tell from headshots other than if they're attractive and hopefully some sense of how old they are.

**MH:** I try to get a good sense of the personality, of who the actor is. I don't like things that are distracting like hands in a three-quarter shot, or distracting clothing or background.

**RY:** The soul. Sexuality. You can tell a lot about somebody in a photo. I'm not concerned about the style of the photo, just that it looks like the person. What makes me go absolutely ballistic is when I call somebody in from a photo and she doesn't look anything at all like her picture. I look for interesting, quirky, offbeat faces.

**BT:** I like the three-quarter shots because they show the body. And now they're doing the photos horizontally, which I personally like the most.

**PM:** It depends on what I'm looking for. It depends on what the needs of the role are. In a feature film, the "look" might be more important than certain skills.

**SH:** I look for a natural quality. I just want the person to look like the photo. No surprises when he walks in the door.

**SS:** I want the photo to look exactly like the actor. I don't want it duped up. I want to see all the lines, all the crevices, the mistakes, the blotches. I don't want actors to idealize themselves.

**CR:** You know, a lot of people choose shots that are down or at unusual angles, and the actor should be centered in the photo.

**AK:** There are what we call "paraplegic" shots where they're holding their arm under them, or hanging out a window, or it looks like they're being strangled. We don't want to see that you can do gymnastics. We prefer the three-quarter shots to the face shot. I think it should be a full bleed; I don't think you should use borders.

**What do you look for on an actor's résumé?**

**SR:** I'm an old-fashioned lady about training. I think an actor should be trained in the classics. I believe in a college education. I hope that the actor has some repertory training. Seven seasons of stock isn't the answer for me.

**RG:** I look for theater. I look for work on movies that I would consider to be quirky, interesting, sexy kind of stuff. I look for work in New York and England. If I'm working on a comedy, I'll look to see if they've done *Saturday Night Live* or Second City or if they've worked with the Groundlings or Exit 57 in New York. That will get me interested. The comedy stuff will speak to me. I want to see who they've trained with. People who have done theater in New York and Chicago usually grab me. That's my background and I feel strongly about it.

**LO:** I want to see if they've done classy movies or shows. I want to see if they've worked with directors I know and respect. Like if they've worked for Barry Levinson who we work with here (*Homicide*), that impresses me. I also look at the training and see who they've studied with. College is very important to me. Yale School of Drama, Carnegie Mellon, and Julliard certainly attract me.

**PG:** I look for a variety of different credits. I'm always looking to see their training. Next I look to see what work they've done in the business and with whom.

**MH:** Primarily, I start with the television and film credits. I want to see what shows they've done, what directors they've worked with. With theater, I look to see if they've done comedy, if they've worked with Second City or an improv group, that kind of thing.

**RY:** The first thing I go to is theater. Then I go to film; what they've done and who they've worked with. Next I look to see where they've studied.

**BT:** I look for some sort of personal connection that I can make. Like some show that I personally saw; a name that I can identify. Like if I knew a director, say Brian Mertes, if his name was on a résumé, I'd have some connection. It's an information tool rather than a credit tool. I always tell actors to put as much as you possibly can on them. You never know who it is we might know. If actors lie on their résumés and I catch them, they begin with a strike against them.

**PM:** The thing about it really is there's no tricks to this, and actors want tricks. It's about being the best person for the job. It really has to come from the training and the background on the résumé. In an ideal world, everybody would get a chance to rehearse the part and play the part and then we'd decide whether we'd want to hire them or not. But that ain't gonna happen. So we're trying to get the best person for the role, given the needs of the producer and the director. Actors have to learn that actors act and directors direct. Directors are not acting coaches who are going to tell them how to play the role. Actors have to know what the actor's responsibilities are. And that includes a variety of ways of playing the role and being flexible.

**SH:** Specific credits that might influence the specific audition. After training I look for major credits.

**SS:** Because of my background in the theater, I look for the training first, but I also look for the experience.

**CR:** I look at it in much the same way that an agent would. I look at the name, contact number, height, and weight on each picture. If that information isn't there I have no idea who they are.

**AK:** I look at theatrical experience. Unless I'm doing a print job where it doesn't matter.

**How do you suggest actors make themselves known to you? What do you recommend they don't do?**

**SR:** For several years what I've been doing is using the office of whichever producer I'm casting for. I don't have an office per se. I limit what I see to recommendations. If someone I respect says, "You must see this actor," I generally will. For instance, when Michael Thomas [the agent] told me about Edward Norton [the actor], he told me I really had to see his work. I went down to the studio where Norton was doing scenes. Then I watched this incredibly gifted young actor do his work. Two other actors, Sean Penn and Robert Downey Jr., also affected me that way. I was delighted to be able to help their careers. Those three are in a class all of their own. Getting back to Edward Norton. Since he wasn't in a play at the time, I asked that he show me everything. I knew that he did dialects, classics. And in that one hour he greatly impressed me.

Over the years I've been all over. I'd go off-off-off if I heard an actor was that special. But I do request that actors not invite me to shows with a lot of profanity or with nudity. It offends me. Also, actors make the mistake of inviting casting people to shows that they're not great in or have very small roles in. What's the point? You shouldn't be that desperate. Actors must be as selective about the showcase they're in as anything else in their careers. I'm not saying that they shouldn't do a showcase just to keep themselves tuned up. Actors must also learn what they're good at and what their limitations are. Getting back to your question. I don't like when actors send me postcards just to tell me they exist.

**RG:** Postcards are a waste of time. I don't even look at them. If people are doing interesting theater work, especially here in L.A. where it's a rarity, that's important to me because I come from a theater background and I respond to that. A snappy flier to the play will get my attention. Don't do those showcases (the ones that you pay to be in). I think they're a waste of time. For me, it's really about networking, but in a creative kind of way. Let's say someone is in a play and he really takes his theater work seriously. Then he gets together with other people and someone knows somebody that works for me. Here's an example, Tracy Villar. I've known of her for a long time and thought she always did good work. She did great work in a *Naked Angels* production out here recently. Everybody I know saw it and talked about it. We talked about it and we brought her in and she did a slam-bam audition for us. Other people had seen her over at Paramount for the movie I'm directing. Now her name has come up seriously for the project and her name is on the list. None of us in this room had seen her in the play, but we all heard how great she was.

**LO:** Don't call me. The best thing an actor can do is to keep working. If you don't have the luxury of working in movies or TV, then in theater.

**PG:** Probably the best thing that they can do is let me know when they're doing a theater piece. Not a scene showcase night. If they're in a film or in something on TV, let me know. Do not send a lot of unsolicited headshots or tapes.

**MH:** The best way is to get into a theater production and send me an invitation with good reviews. I go to theater, comedy clubs, and improv groups. If I get a photo and the look is unique, that could get me interested in the actor. I look at all my mail. What I don't like is actors stopping by. Some actors think that constant phone calls are good— they're not!

**RY:** I recommend they don't call unless I know them. I suggest they send a picture and résumé and a letter. If they know somebody who knows me, mention it (and be truthful).

We just can't be inundated with a thousand calls. If it's somebody that I know and she wants me to see something she's in, then I suggest she call. I can make a plan to see her right there.

**BT:** If it's an actor I don't know, I suggest writing me a really good business letter introducing himself to me. I get a hundred to two hundred résumés a day. Let's assume they're all people introducing themselves to me. Well, if there's nothing on the credits that's going to make the résumé stand out, then obviously a really good letter of introduction with what it is the actor is specifically looking for is more effective than the general "hire me." For instance, if someone writes something very specific, like if she says, I'm new to New York, I graduated from so-and-so, I have no agent representation, and I'm aware that you cast *Food Chain* and if you're ever casting an understudy for Hope Davis I'd love to be seen for it. That automatically let's me know that that woman has a clue, as opposed to just a blanket résumé in the mail that says "Hire me," or "I want to replace Hope Davis." I mean the person that asks to be seen for the understudy already shows to me that she knows. Obviously, it doesn't mean she doesn't want to be the replacement, but she knows there's a million working actresses that we know already that will probably get that part.

Lying or crashing an audition are things I really dislike.

**PM:** I become interested in people by seeing their work. I don't like actors who try tricks to get my attention. Deal with me at a professional level through my office. Postcards and fliers are still the best way to keep in touch, to let me know what you're doing.

**SH:** The difficult thing, of course, is that they have to have work for us to see them. I don't think it's wrong if you're an understudy, for instance, and you're only going on today, to call us. You obviously can't wait to go through the mail. Mailing is always the best. I don't like actors who call for no reason. Many actors have the mistaken notion that when we hear their names, if they call enough, we'll audition them. I think it's the opposite. It's a turnoff. Actors I don't know who send me postcards are wasting their time.

**SS:** The first Monday of every month we have an open audition for two hours. The first twenty people that sign up for this open call get seen. For Equity actors there is the LORT lottery. I see a lot of actors like that. One thing I don't want is actors to call me. Actors open themselves up to be hurt sometimes. They can call here and have no idea what I'm doing, what I might be in the middle of. I may not feel well, may be in an argument with a director. If they call then, they'll get the brunt of it.

**CR:** Don't phone. Postcards are the best way. Original submissions should be eight-by-tens. Then after that, follow up with postcards.

**AK:** And then if you're in a show, send us a flier. And don't forget to highlight your name so we know who sent it.

**What determines whether or not you'll see an actor in a show?**

**SR:** As I've mentioned, I won't see a show with nudity or with profanity. I only go if there's a strong recommendation by someone I totally trust. If someone from my past sends me a flier and I've always loved their work, perhaps I will go. But mainly to Off-Broadway. Very rarely do I see showcases.

**RG:** I don't see that many shows anymore. But people in my office do. It depends on whether the show is classy. New work is good. Doing a revival of *Barefoot in the Park* is not going to get much attention.

**LO:** Within my casting department here at NBC, there's me and three other casting directors. We see as much as we can. One of the casting directors goes to the comedy clubs. And the other two cover a lot. I watch a lot of TV. I look to see on the flier if the play has a good director, a writer I like. If the show is too far away, I probably won't be able to go.

**PG:** If it's a show with a relatively large cast, I'm more prone to be interested. If it's a theater group that I know or admire or if it's a director or writer whose work I like. I'm generally more inclined to see a comedy than a drama.

**MH:** Something that strikes me personally about the show, or word of mouth on it, or good reviews. Other things are if it's a play I haven't seen by a director I like; if there's another actor in the cast whose work I like; if it's a writer I like. All of those things affect my decision.

**RY:** In New York I used to go to the theater six times a week, not out here. If it's a good play and there's good word of mouth on it, I'll go. I'll go to the Mark Taper, good plays, like that. I'm a single parent, I can't be out a lot.

**BT:** Timing, how interested I am in that actor, or how interested I am in that show. I go to shows that have a lot of actors I don't know in them. If a show has a lot of young men in it and I'm presently casting a production of *Biloxi Blues*, the timing is right. If a show has a lot of Latinos in it and I'm casting a Latino play, I'll go.

**PM:** They have to do projects that are of interest to a casting director— a play with a lot of actors in it; an interesting writer; a good acting company; a safe locale [where it's produced]. We're always looking for new people. But you have to remember that casting directors are human beings. They put in long, stressful days, and they have to be treated as professionals.

**SH:** I think mostly we like to see new plays. There are some companies that have good names. I'm not going to go to an address that I'm frightened of, that's for damn sure. Companies such as MCC, York, Atlantic, WPA. In our office I send the assistants and interns to the school class nights such as AMDA, and Circle in the Square School.

**SS:** I go to the theater if I can. Quite often I don't go to just see an actor, I go to see a show. I'll read a review that'll peak my interest. I always tell actors I know, "If you're doing something let me know. If I can fit it in, I will go."

**CR:** The length of the showcase is very important. If it's going to go on for three-and-a-half hours, and it's hot, and there's no air-conditioning, forget it.

**AK:** We won't see *Hamlet*.

**CR:** The opposite is true. If it's cold and there's no heat in the theater, forget about it. Just keep it short and sweet. We can tell within the first few minutes whether you have talent or not.

**AK:** I like the scenes nights because they usually start at 6:00 or 6:30 P.M.; you're out of there in time to have a decent evening. Also, I get to see twenty people in an hour. A flier that's different can get me to see a show. An oddball show might get my interest. I recently got a flier for *The Cabinet of Doctor Caligari.* Now I thought that's interesting, and I went. Something like drag queens in outer space, that sounds good. I'll go to that. It could be funny, as opposed to the standards like *Our Town* or *Romeo and Juliet.*

### Do you have any specific actor do's and don'ts (pet peeves)?

**SR:** At open calls at Actors Equity, when actors are totally wrong for a part and come to the call "just to meet me," that's wrong. Also, don't talk a lot. Just come in, say hello, do the audition, say thank you, and leave. No excuses, no apologies, please. Don't come to an audition and say, "I have a cold and can't sing well today." If that's the case, cancel the audition. Don't waste our time. Dressing for the part isn't a bad idea [within reason]. If that helps the actor to feel better for the part, then I feel he should. After I've told you everything I know about the character, if you feel the need to ask the director what he has in mind for the part, I think you absolutely should. When actors would ask Frank Perry [the late film director] what he had in mind for the character, he'd say, "I'll tell you after." He never did, of course. If an actor can be extremely creative with what he sees in the moment, there is a magical audition. When Sean Penn auditioned for the movie *Taps,* he was really not what we had in mind. They were looking for a Philip Barry type. His agent Mary Harden begged us to please see him. And I trusted her taste. Well, Sean made choices at that audition, was incredibly creative, won me over. He thought of all these things to do. I remember he had this soft-drink can and made such interesting choices, such interesting behavior for that character. It blew my mind. I rushed him to Stanley Jaffe and said you must see. Long story short— he got the part and a career took off.

**RG:** Stopping by doesn't work at all. Actors calling me at home isn't a good idea either. I don't like getting accosted in the supermarket. I used to get accosted in New York a lot in the lobbies of plays or in bars. It's not as bad out here. Being overly aggressive and stalking are also things I don't like. People can be very desperate here.

**LO:** I don't like being stalked or approached in a restaurant unless you really know me. We make ourselves fairly accessible here in the office but outside, please, no. The obvious things like being prepared and being on time are always important for actors to know.

**PG:** To me, it's all about sincerity. I'd rather have an actor be quiet and reserved than overly showy. To the extent that I can gauge, I'd like to see that they're being themselves.

**MH:** The thing that's most infuriating is actors who show up for an audition unprepared. Especially when they had a script available to them and didn't bother or have time to work on it. It wastes everyone's time. Also, actors who show up late, or forgot their pictures and résumés; things like that. Something I like is when an actor keeps the audition simple, doesn't complicate it.

**RY:** I love when actors are prepared. I love when they do their homework. When they're given a script and they go home and take the time to get into the character, create a life. I love to see them come into the audition having made choices. I don't like when an actor doesn't do his homework and sort of wings it. He must take care of his craft, his voice. Do all the things that will make him a better actor. I like people who take chances, who don't care what people think.

**BT:** Be as prepared as you can possibly be for an audition. I watch too many actors pick up the sides five minutes before an audition or not know what the right sides were. If we can be prepared to get the appointments out a day or two or sometimes up to a week before an audition, you want the actor to be prepared. It's such a waste of time when someone says at an audition, "I didn't get a chance to read the play." There's not enough time to see everyone at an audition as it is. Also, don't blow off an audition. If you can't come, cancel an audition.

**PM:** I hate when actors are unprepared. I hate excuses. I'm not happy when actors don't update their phone numbers, don't update their union contacts. That drives me crazy.

**SH:** I can't bear when actors put their postcards in Christmas cards. If I don't know you, why are you sending me a Christmas card? My real major, major pet peeve is actors who don't take the profession seriously. Actors who are unprepared, late. When I was at Ogilvy & Mather a long time ago, we did, in conjunction with the union, a survey. We found out that 41 percent of actors are late for auditions. Forty-one percent! And we're not talking three minutes here. When I first came into this business, whether for a commercial, a play, a movie, you always came early. You should be there with enough time to get yourself into a good place, emotionally. To prepare. I would say seven out of ten actors come in two seconds before their auditions to fifteen minutes late. Also, I should mention I very much admire strong choices.

**SS:** The audition is the most important thing. The work is the most important thing. Social chat that's provoked at the audition by the actor wastes everybody's time. Only ask questions at the audition if you have to. Make your questions succinct. The major thing the director wants to see is your work. If the director wants to talk to you, let him start the conversation. No needless questions! Dress classically. Dress well, nice. Dress near to the part if you want to, but don't look like you just came from a costume shop. And for God's sake, the only props you should bring in are hand props that you can take out with you. And don't bring in changes of clothing.

**CR:** Actors should come prepared. They should be ready to do the work. They should come in, prepare, and not socialize. Take the script, make some choices. So when your name is called, you are really ready to go in. In an audition situation, I need to move people. According to the union regulations, I have an hour to get you in and out. Also, I rent studios based on what I'm doing. I don't need people wasting time. Be aware that I'm not there to be your buddy.

**AK:** Something that really bothers me is actors who don't leave. They just linger. Finally, you go to the door and open it and they're still standing there. We have your picture, we met, you've been auditioned—now leave.

**CR:** To get back to socializing. Most studios that you rent are not well equipped as far as soundproofing. So if you're talking, and joking and laughing, it all bleeds through the door and interrupts what I'm doing. Also, don't berate yourself. Don't tell me that this is a terrible picture or complain about how your résumé isn't updated yet. Don't whine or tell me that this was just a little role in such-and-such a play.

### When interviewing an actor, what do you look for?

**SR:** In the old days I used to interview actors all the time for a film. These days hardly ever. Just some basic things. Be on time, please. I have a thing about punctuality. Excuses of any kind are not smart at an interview. No apologies. Just try to be open, friendly, and, most of all, present yourself as a professional, not as a kid.

**RG:** Presence, self-assurance, confidence, a positive attitude.

**LO:** There's a natural charisma that you find where you know it's just going to happen for these people. I met Julia Roberts and Meg Ryan early on in their careers. Julia just glowed when she walked in; Meg had a special presence you couldn't miss.

**PG:** Again, I look for sincerity, for commitment to their craft. A big turnoff for me is actors who say, "I'm not interested in stage work. I just want to work in TV and film."

There's something very organic about an actor who comes in the room and let's down whatever mask she may be wearing. I know that she feels that there's a lot riding on it. And that's why general interviews are really more valuable to me if I've seen the actor's work.

**MH:** I have general interviews, but I don't find them as valuable as a specific audition. I'm very open at the interview. I respond to the actor just like I'd respond to meeting someone in a personal situation. Is he interesting to me? Does he have anything else going on in his life besides being an actor? I like actors who are also artists and musicians, who have a life. I like to see if they're smart, intelligent, well rounded.

**RY:** Humor. I love somebody who's just down-to-earth, is funny, and that I can relate to. I like actors who I can just hang out with, talk about anything.

**BT:** Once a week I interview actors. I always look for something that will connect me to the actor. I like to see a person who has a sense of himself. I look for a personality. It's still a people business. It's not just talent or looks.

**PM:** Half the time actors come in, they have no idea who you are. They have no idea what projects you work on. We have to do our homework about the actors; they should do some about us. No one wanders into IBM and asks, What do you do here? You see it's very easy to fail as an actor, because it's hard to succeed. The options are so limited. If there is a specific project I'm casting that they're interested in, they should bring it to my attention. Usually, I know what it is.

**SH:** It's a whole other craft, being interviewed. The ability to sell yourself by being honest, straightforward, simple. And charm doesn't hurt. Too many actors don't know who they are. They interview like accountants. They sit there and want you to ask them questions. They don't know how to present themselves. I think the worst kind of interviewee is a passive interviewee.

**SS:** I'm looking to see them as people. I know that it may be hard, but I want them to just be themselves. Actors don't need to feel that it's just them who need to control the conversation. If they're dealing with someone who's decent in this business, they'll provoke the conversation. It's really up to the casting director to ask you where you're from, what you want to do, what your ambitions are, what you've been in. You only have to be agile in the way you answer questions. Don't feel that the whole responsibility for the interview comes from you. Unfortunately, there are a lot of casting directors out there who don't realize what I'm saying and they put the actor on the spot.

**CR:** I'm looking for someone who is very much there. I want a firm handshake and look me in the eyes. And the minute I open the door to ask a question—just take off. I'm not sitting there with people who are waiting for me to take their personality out. I need to ask just one question like, "I see you did so-and-so. How was it?" Then bam! The actor should just take off. Tell me about your favorite role. What are your dream roles? Be ready to be talkative.

**AK:** What we really look for is presence. Many actors seem to get so insecure, so bent out of shape. Inside their heads they're thinking, "Oh my God, do I look good?" "Oh my God, do they think I'm smart?" "Oh my God, am I saying the right thing?!" Although something else is coming out of their mouths, you're just hearing what's going on in their heads (because they're feeling so insecure). There's more than one job, let's face it. When I was an actor, I thought every audition was going to be my last. This is long-term. Also, I like a sense of humor.

### When auditioning actors, what do you look for?

**SR:** The most important thing you must remember is that casting directors are looking for a quality—not a performance. Be creative. As I mentioned before, Sean Penn came in for *Taps* and showed us something entirely different, something that wasn't on the page. We can read; we know what the script says. It's the actor who's daring and comes in with something above what's on the page and makes fully committed choices. Of course, I must see an actor who can relate to the character. Just to go out on a limb is not enough if you don't know the inside of the character on the page. You must be able to expand what is on the page, enlarge it. I always read with the actors who audition for me. I've never hired a reader in my whole career.

**RG:** I look for someone who is really all about the work, not about all the bullshit. I want to see someone who's focused on the work and has a real sense of himself. It's amazing how people sabotage themselves. They say things like, "I just got this yesterday and didn't have a chance to look at it." Or "I didn't have a chance to read the script." Or "What are you guys looking for?" When people start just chatting, it gets kind of stupid.

**LO:** Talent! Knowing how to make a scene work, how to make themselves believable. Adding something to the scene that others didn't. Actors should make strong, definite choices and go with them. And, at the same time, they should be accessible to directions if they're given an adjustment.

**PG:** I look for actors who are listening to their auditioning partners or to the reader. A big don't for me for actors is to have the words so memorized that it's all mechanical. They wait a specific amount of time before they respond, etc. It's all too rehearsed, too planned, not spontaneous or in the moment. I like to read with actors because they're paying attention to what I'm saying. And if I take a beat between a certain line reading and they've jumped over my words, it's because they're so rehearsed in it. Nerves, particularly by the time they get to a network, is something that we have to take into consideration. I always look for previous work that the actor has done that I can show to the executives if I feel that his audition didn't come off well. If I've seen that actor in a film project or in TV or theater and he doesn't hit it in the room, I'll do everything I can to help him. With those actors whose work I know and who don't audition well, I try to come to bat for them with the executives by saying things like, "This actor just doesn't audition well. Listen to the voice. Does the height work for you? Does the age work for you? Physically is he the right type? You're not going to see it in the audition. I know this actor's work though." A lot of actors look at the audition as a work-in-progress. There's an immediacy about television. The time from when an audition takes place to when a role needs to be cast to getting the show on the air is so small. Sometimes wonderful actors need to speed up the process that they'd usually take. At an audition where an actor might just be getting comfortable in the idea of what the role is, he's expected to give a finished performance. But the reality of doing TV is actors are constantly given new pages just minutes before they're about to shoot the scene. At these auditions, actors are lucky to be given the scenes the day before the audition.

**MH:** I look to see if the actor has a clear understanding of the character. I want to see strong, intelligent choices. Do they understand the context of the scene? Actors don't need to bring in props for the audition. Also, don't work on a lot of blocking; it's unnecessary. Some actors think if they fumble over a few lines, they've blown the audition. The words are the least important part.

**RY:** It depends. Sometimes actors are in character when they come into an audition. If I can pick that up, if I get that, I'll tell the director,

"Let's just go into it and you can talk after." I like it when an actor tells me that he'd rather talk after if he's already in character. Although some directors like to chat first, if I see the actor's in character, I let them know we'll talk after. I always provide actors as readers so you always have somebody to read off of. At the audition I'm looking for choices, for colors, for layers. As I said, I love actors who take chances, make choices that are interesting, and go for it. Also, you always look for the actor who didn't make the obvious choice. Humor, even in a scene that may not call for it, can add a lot. Humor can encapsulate a lot and it really endears you to people.

**BT:** You look to see if they're prepared, if they have a sense of the project they're auditioning for. During the audition, you're looking for the actor who can perform this role, has all the emotional colors necessary to do this part. The actor who takes that audition scene and can make it as colorful as the whole two-hour play or movie is a real find.

**PM:** I want them to be good. I look for the actor who knows what he's doing, is professional. You want to feel the actor knows what the material is about. I really hate when an actor comes in, is introduced to the director, and seems befuddled. It's a profession, a business. A lot of young actors just think it's art.

**SH:** Strong choices. It takes a while to see if someone is a yes, but the no is instantaneous. I look for someone who comes into the room and heats it up. And usually that happens more often with women. Men are, by and large, more closed.

**SS:** Simply put, they must show me that they can do the role. I don't have a set pattern of what I look for. The most important thing is the work. That's what the focus is. We want you to get the job. We certainly didn't bring you in so that you'll be terrible.

**CR:** Creativity and choices. Be the life of the party. Make us believe you know what you're doing. Even if you don't, make us believe you do. You come into the audition with as much confidence as you can and make us believe that that script was written for you.

## How do you prefer actors maintain contact with your office? How often?

**SR:** Since I don't have an office, there is nowhere to send mail to. There are those people whose work I know very well that let me know what's going on in their careers. If they are in something good, they let me know by mailing me fliers to my apartment. But I don't like mail from people I don't know.

**RG:** If they have an agent or manager, it should be through them.

**LO:** I like the postcards telling me what they're doing. The best way is though their representatives, their agents or managers.

**PG:** If they have a good agent, the agent will make sure that they're in our minds. If they're not represented, once in a while a postcard. On this subject of not being represented, most of the actors I see are represented by agents. Because I'm not online casting, I'm responsible for overall casting of everything on our network. When I worked for Stephen Cannell casting *Wiseguys*, or when I was in New York casting *The Cosby Show*, I would see many actors that weren't represented. I'd say about 50 percent of the actors that I saw for *Cosby* weren't represented. The people who cover specific areas in my department— Michael Katcher who covers the comedies, Lucy Kavallo who covers the dramas, and Fern Ornstein who covers the movies of the week— tend to see many more actors than I do. Many of those actors are not represented.

**MH:** I like when actors send me postcards telling me they're in an episode of such-and-such, or this movie, or this play. Even if I can't catch the show, I get a sense of awareness that they're working. Hearing from an actor once every month or two is fine. But just dropping me a line saying "Hey remember me?" is really not too productive. If you have something to tell me about, that's the best time—even from an actor I don't know. If I get a card from an actor I don't know letting me know "I'm appearing on *Murphy Brown,* or in this play," it peaks my curiosity about him or her. Maybe I should get to know them.

**RY:** Notes. I move around a lot, go from job to job. We don't have a permanent office yet. Once I get my permanent office, I know I'll be inundated. But I do like personal notes, people filling me in on what they're doing. But actors should only contact me when they have something monumental to tell me. If it's somebody I know, however, I like to know what's going on with them.

**BT:** I think maintaining contact with the office is very important. It may have been someone I worked with a while back and just forgot. I look at every piece of mail. Postcards are very good ways. Every eight to twelve weeks is a good amount of time since you're always starting a new project about every two months. Unless it's commercials, which we do every week. I encourage actors to keep in touch. That postcard that comes in at the right moment, just when you're looking for that type—bam! Get her in tomorrow for the Maxwell House commercial! or it might be—Get her in tomorrow for *The Three Sisters* at Hartford. It's okay to say, "Just keeping in touch. Anything you're presently casting that I might be right for?"

**PM:** Postcards. Or when they're doing something. If you're on a soap, let me know. I may not have to see the soap, but at least I know you're working.

**SH:** I don't mind the postcards. I don't mind the notes. I think they all work.

**SS:** Postcards, but please don't inundate me. If you're in a showcase, let me know about it. Only contact me, at most, once a month or so.

**CR:** Postcards, once a month.

**AK:** This once-a-week stuff just makes me crazy.

**If you had just one tip to give an actor regarding his career, what would it be?**

**SR:** Study. Training. I can't think of anything else that's important. One piece of advice for singers for musicals—be sure that the song that you sing is within your range without the break in the voice. Never sing something that you haven't studied and studied.

**RG:** Act every day. In class, in workshops, in the theater, making short films for friends. Anything you can do—just keep acting.

**LO:** Be prepared before you start the auditioning process. You can make a lot of bad connections. The way to determine when you're ready is in your acting classes and just a feeling that I'm ready, it's time. Don't enter the business too soon—it can be very damaging.

**PG:** Act because you can't not act. If you can do something else, then do it. An actor I know once said that the reason he loved auditioning is because it was another opportunity to perform and he loved to perform. He was lucky just to have an opportunity to audition. Getting the roles were the best thing, icing on the cake. My advice is take any opportunity you can get to perform. If it means working on a student film. If it means working in a small theater group somewhere. These days there are no limits to where a casting director will go to find talent. In terms of supply and demand, the demand is so high. In television, the six networks, as well as many cable channels, are constantly looking for new talent. Also, always remember acting is a craft that is a combination of instinct and training.

**MH:** Take charge of your career yourself. Don't completely hand it over to an agent or manager and wait by the phone. The whole idea of an actor signing with a manager just to have additional doors open, I don't think it's too smart. A lot of actors sign with managers and don't even know who the manager's other clients are. Ask yourself, What can this manager do for me that my agent couldn't do? It's an unawareness of what their representation is doing for them.

**RY:** Study. Study, study, study, study. And with good people. Always just work with good people. Do theater as much as you can in between. And don't give up. If it's what you want more than anything in the world, and it has to be what you want more than anything else in the world—don't give up!

**BT:** I have two tips. One is you must understand it's a business. Treat any communication and contact in that way. Treat it the same as if you were going for a job at IBM. The second thing is keep yourself constantly involved in a creative atmosphere. That doesn't mean you have to go to the extreme of starting your own theater company, but start your own Monday night reading series. Constantly do something creative. Don't spend all your time on self-promotion and losing your art. Do something creative at least once a week. Also, actors should always remember that casting directors are really on their side. We want them to give a great audition.

**PM:** Train and keep training. Keep those juices flowing. Because it's always changing and there's so much that you have to have a background on. Actors should keep working whether it's showcases or classes.

**SH:** Don't stop studying. I think it's important to work. Geraldine Page never stopped. After she got through with Lee Strassberg, she went to Uta Hagen (or maybe it was the other way around).

**SS:** Take it seriously. You're the product and you're only as good as the product you've made. You're only as good as how much you've invested in it. If you want to do this, only do it because you have no other choices. Don't do this to get a swimming pool and a car and all the rest of that stuff. Only get into this business if it's the only thing in your life and you don't want to do anything else.

**AK:** Mine is, Don't quit your straight job. Have something else to do. There will be months when you're not acting and what are you going to do, sit there and look at the telephone?

**CR:** Try to be two people in your career. Be the actor, the creative person, and also be the businessperson. You have to do the things that are appropriate to get the auditions. Get into a network to meet people within the industry. Be the businessperson who can sell herself. If you can't be a businessperson then hire a manager or work your butt off to get an agent.

**AK:** There are great trade-offs. Back when I started out, I made friends with this fabulous singer. I was a character singer but I needed voice lessons and I couldn't afford them. She needed acting lessons and I was a very good actress, so we traded. I gave her coaching lessons and she helped me with my voice, and it didn't cost either of us anything.

# About the Author

**G**LENN ALTERMAN is the author of *Street Talk (Original Character Monologues for Actors)*, *Uptown*, *Two Minutes and Under*, *The Job Book— 100 Acting Jobs for Actors*, *The Job Book 2—100 Day Jobs for Actors*, and *What to Give Your Agent for Christmas (And 100 Other Helpful Hints for Working Actors)* published by Smith & Kraus. *Street Talk* and *Uptown* were the number one bestselling books of original monologues in 1992 and 1993, and, along with *The Job Book—100 Acting Jobs for Actors* and *The Job Book 2—100 Day Jobs for Actors*, were featured selections in the Doubleday Book Club (Fireside Theater and Stage and Screen book clubs). *Two Minutes and Under* recently went into its second printing. His plays *Like Family* and *The Pecking Order* were optioned by Red Eye Pictures (with Alterman writing the screenplay). *Nobody's Flood* won the Bloomington National Playwriting Competition (finalist in the Key West Theater Festival), *Coulda-Woulda-Shoulda* won the Three Genres Playwriting Competition (including publication in the Prentice Hall college textbook). He wrote the book for *Heartstrings—The National Tour* (commissioned by the Design Industries Foundation for AIDS), a thirty-five city tour that starred Michelle Pfeiffer, Ron Silver, Christopher Reeve, Susan Sarandon, Marlo Thomas, and Sandy

Duncan. Other plays include *Kiss Me When It's Over* (commissioned by E. Weissman Productions), starring and directed by André DeShields, *Tourists of the Mindfield* (semifinalist in the L. Arnold Weissberger Playwriting Competition at New Dramatists), and *Street Talk/Uptown* (based on his books), produced at the West Coast Ensemble in Los Angeles. *Goin' Round on Rock Solid Ground* and *Unfamiliar Faces* were finalists at the Actors Theater of Louisville. *Spilt Milk* received its premiere at Beverly Hills Rep. (Theater 40) and was selected to participate in the Samuel French One Act Play Festival. *The Danger of Strangers* won Honorable Mention in both the Deep South Writers Conference Competition and the Pittsburgh New Works Festival, and was also a finalist in the George R. Kernodle Contest (with productions at Circle Rep. Lab and the West Bank Cafe Downstairs Theater Bar). His plays have been performed at Primary Stages, Circle in the Square (Downtown), HOME, in the Turnip Festival at the Duplex, Playwrights Horizons, La Mama, on Theater Row (in New York City), and at many theaters around the country. He is a member of the Dramatists Guild, the Authors Guild, the National Writers Union, Participating Artists at the Cherry Lane Theater, Circle Rep. Lab, and the Lab Theater Company.

His latest monologue book, *Two Minute Monologues,* was recently published by Merewether publishers.

# Index

## Books from Allworth Press

**An Actor's Guide—Your First Year in Hollywood**
by Michael Saint Nicholas (softcover, 6 × 9, 256 pages, $16.95)

**Writing Scripts Hollywood Will Love**
by Katherine Atwell Herbert (softcover, 6 × 9, 160 pages, $12.95)

**The Performing Arts Business Encyclopedia**
by Leonard DuBoff (softcover, 6 × 9, 256 pages, $19.95)

**Stage Fright: Health & Safety in the Theater**
by Monona Rossol (softcover, 6 × 9, 144 pages, $16.95)

**The Interactive Music Handbook: The Definitive Guide to Internet Music Strategies, Enhanced CD Production, and Business Development** by Jodi Summers (softcover, 6 × 9, 296 pages, $19.95)

**Booking and Tour Management for the Performing Arts**
by Rena Shagan (softcover, 6 × 9, 272 pages, $19.95)

**The Copyright Guide: A Friendly Guide for Protecting and Profiting from Copyrights** by Lee Wilson (softcover, 6 × 9, 192 pages, $18.95)

**The Business of Multimedia** by Nina Schuyler
(softcover, 6 × 9, 240 pages, $19.95)

**The Internet Research Guide** by Timothy K. Maloy
(softcover, 6 × 9, 208 pages, $18.95)

**The Secret Life of Money: How Money Can Be Food for the Soul**
by Tad Crawford, (softcover, 5¹/₂ × 8¹/₂, 304 pages, $14.95)

**Legal-Wise°: Self-Help Legal Guide for Everyone,** Third Edition
by Carl W. Battle (softcover, 8¹/₂ × 11, 208 pages, $18.95)

**Artists Communities** by the Alliance of Artists' Communities
(softcover, 6³/₄ × 10, 224 pages, $16.95)

Please write to request our free catalogue. To order by credit card, call 1-800-491-2808 or send a check or money order to Allworth Press, 10 East 23rd Street, Suite 210, New York, NY 10010. Include $5 for shipping and handling for the first book ordered and $1 for each additional book. Ten dollars plus $1 for each additional book if ordering from Canada. New York State residents must add sales tax.

If you would like to see our complete catalogue on the World Wide Web, you can find us at *www.allworth.com*